# Monster
# LOYALTY

# Monster
# LOYALTY

How
**LADY GAGA**
Turns Followers
into Fanatics

## Jackie Huba

Portfolio / Penguin

PORTFOLIO / PENGUIN
Published by the Penguin Group
Penguin Group (USA) Inc., 375 Hudson Street,
New York, New York 10014, USA

USA | Canada | UK | Ireland | Australia | New Zealand | India | South Africa | China

Penguin Books Ltd, Registered Offices: 80 Strand, London WC2R 0RL, England
For more information about the Penguin Group visit penguin.com

Illustration credits
Page 22: Forrester Research, Inc.
24, 54, and 55: Jackie Huba (designed by Penguin Group (USA) Inc.)
52: Simon Sinek, Inc.
57: Millward Brown Optimor and The Jim Stengel Company
94: AP Photo / Matt Sayles
99: Jason Reeves
110: Jay Directo / AFP / Getty Images
113: Courtesy of Joel Diaz
115: Jackie Huba
127: Courtesy of Gary Sim
134: Rod Brooks and Sean McDonald
151: Krista Kennell / Sipa Press / AP Images
157: Innocent Drinks

Library of Congress Cataloging-in-Publication Data

Huba, Jackie.
    Monster loyalty : how Lady Gaga turns followers into fanatics / Jackie Huba.
        pages cm
    Includes bibliographical references and index.
    ISBN 978-1-59184-650-5
    1. Customer loyalty—Case studies. 2. Customer relations. 3. Marketing—Social
aspects. 4. Lady Gaga. I. Title.
    HF5415.5.H83 2013
    658.8'343—dc23
                        2013006819

Printed in the United States of America
1   3   5   7   9   10   8   6   4   2

Set in Sabon LT Std
Book design by Elyse Strongin

**For Little Monsters**

*Your bravery in the face of society's pressures inspires us all.*

# CONTENTS

Introduction                                  1

From Stefani to Gaga                          9

**LESSON 1**

Focus on Your One Percenters                 19

**LESSON 2**

Lead with Values                             35

**LESSON 3**

Build Community                              67

**LESSON 4**

Give Fans a Name                             91

**LESSON 5**

Embrace Shared Symbols                      105

**LESSON 6**

Make Them Feel Like Rock Stars 121

**LESSON 7**

Generate Something to Talk About 141

Building Monster Loyalty of Your Own 163

Acknowledgments 177
Notes 181
Selected Resources 203
Index 205
About the Author 213

# Monster
# LOYALTY

# Introduction

"Dear Mama Monster,

No one has been here for me like you have for the last few years. You change millions of peoples' [*sic*] lives and for that and so many other reasons, you are a true inspiration . . . You show that it is ok to be different and that if you have a dream, you should not stop until you reach it. I not only see you as a singer, Gaga, I see you as a way of life . . .

**love, your little monster, Bree <3"**

**W**ith fan letters like this pouring in every day, it's no wonder Lady Gaga is one of the most well-known pop artists in the world. A fan base that spans the globe and an estimated 23 million albums and 64 million singles sold worldwide also make her one of the best-selling music artists of all time. Her achievements include five Grammy Awards, thirteen MTV Video Music Awards, consecutive appearances on *Billboard* magazine's Artists of the Year (scoring the definitive Best Artist overall title in 2010), a ranking of fourth on VH1's list of 100 Greatest Women in Music, and a spot on *Time* magazine's 2010 list of the 100 Most Influential People in the World. In 2011, she was ranked No. 1 on *Billboard*'s list of top moneymakers, grossing more than $30 million. That same year *Forbes* named her the world's most powerful celebrity, ahead of Oprah Winfrey. When you overtake Oprah Winfrey on any list, clearly you have a large amount of power and influence.

But Lady Gaga didn't become the success she is solely based on talent, which she certainly has in spades. She did so by engendering immense loyalty in fans, not just through her music, but with the message she inspires and the community she has built around it. To anyone in the business community, this sounds like a classic case of loyalty marketing and customer cultivation—and it is. Lady Gaga is not just a pop star; she is an incredible businessperson.

I first became a Gaga fan in 2009 when I was drawn in by the addictive dance beats of her first album *The Fame*. Yet the more I watched how she interacted with her fans, the more impressed I became with how she methodically created her passionate fan base. I saw her relate to her fans on a much more intimate level than most of her ego-driven contemporaries did. Fans were pouring their hearts out online, not just about how much they loved Gaga's music and fashion, but also about how she had inspired them to be better people. I wanted to know how she was inspiring such devotion. I read every article I could find about her and pored through interviews she had given to print and television outlets. I started following her on Facebook, where she has the third-highest number of fans with 55 million, and on Twitter, where she is the most followed with more than 33 million followers, as well as on Tumblr and other social sites. I watched grainy, tinny-sounding videos of her performances and concerts uploaded to YouTube by fans around the world. I visited the top Gaga fan sites daily to see what they were reporting and what fans were saying on the forums. I've even been to three of her concerts. What I began to see amazed me. Lady Gaga is doing something casual observers and many business professionals may not really comprehend. While creating a buzz with her wild outfits and crazy performance art, she is methodically building a grassroots base of passionate fans for the long term. The more I observed, the more I began to realize that there is a lot she could teach the business world about how to generate customer loyalty.

I first wrote about this topic in February 2010 for my blog, *Church of the Customer*, with a post entitled "Loyalty Lessons from Lady Gaga." It was the most retweeted and passed-along post I had ever written in my seven years of blogging. When celebrity gossip blogger Perez Hilton retweeted it, I realized that I was on to something big. I began adding Lady Gaga as a case study in my keynote speaking and got a terrific response from my audiences. People told me they hadn't realized all of the things she was doing to engage fans and that learning about her as a person and what she has accomplished helps them think about their own customers in a different way. The largest consumer packaged-good companies in the world, such as Coca-Cola, benchmark Gaga instead of their competitors for how she engages her fans on social media. Technology companies, like Austin, Texas–based Bazaarvoice, have looked for inspiration by inviting Gaga's manager to speak to their entire workforce about how she connects with fans. After I became well versed in Gaga's fan loyalty, BBC Radio in London interviewed me about her marketing abilities when her third album, *Born This Way*, was released in May 2011. It was then that the idea for this book was born. I call it *Monster Loyalty* because I want to detail the business of how to create "Little Monster"-like customers (as I'll explain more about later, "Little Monsters" is the name Lady Gaga has given her fans). And I want to encourage readers to create Monster Loyalty within their own businesses and organizations.

Lady Gaga's business sense impresses me, but her passion for changing the world for the better through any means possible is what truly inspired me to study her. She is influencing an entire generation of young people to stand up for one another, to be more tolerant of differences, and to be brave in the face of difficulty. I have spent hours and hours reading fan comments about how she has changed lives for the better. I have cried watching YouTube videos of kids saying they thought about hurting themselves or ending their lives, but that her belief in them, a woman they don't even know, kept them from doing it. They listen to her music, especially "Born This Way," and they feel better about themselves. You will learn more about what she is doing by reading this book. But part of why I wanted to write it is that I am compelled to share all of the things she is doing, not just her business acumen. I believe that if there was ever a candidate to continue Oprah's legacy of inspiring people to live their best lives, it's this five-foot-one, twenty-six-year-old in a studded bikini.

I didn't work with Lady Gaga or anyone on Gaga's extended team at the Haus of Gaga in the creation of this book. My inspiration comes from the same genuine place that causes so many of her fans to want to express themselves for who they are. I see the world through the lens of business and marketing and I believe that the same things Lady Gaga intuitively does can help anyone connect with their customers and create a tribe as passionate as the Little Monsters. I am an evangelist for creating passionate customer loyalty. This has been a thread through all of my previous books and continues in this one.

Lady Gaga certainly is not the type of person (or concept) that commercial businesses usually benchmark. Her crazy stage performances, during which she lights a piano on fire or pops out of an egg, and her weird outfits, such as the infamous meat dress, create a smoke screen that masks a more serious business sense. Behind that smoke screen, though, Gaga uses intuitive customer strategies that more conventional businesses would do well to study and employ. By exploring Lady Gaga's biography, her fan philosophy, and the seven key loyalty lessons I have discovered, this book provides a complete case study that can be a model to help companies large and small build, maintain, and expand the core customer base crucial to their success. For each of Gaga's loyalty lessons, I will illustrate examples of how businesses are applying that lesson. At the end of the book, I'll give you a schema and provide a worksheet of sorts to get you thinking about how to build Monster Loyalty of your own. As most businesspeople know, and as Lady Gaga's bio in the next chapter will show, the best ideas sometimes come from the unlikeliest sources.

## From Stefani to Gaga

"When I wake up in the morning, I feel like any other insecure 24-year-old girl. Then I say, 'Bitch, you're Lady Gaga, you get up and walk the walk today.'"

—Lady Gaga, June 2010

Lady Gaga has become a model loyalty marketer at the tender age of twenty-six. The strategies and tactics she has used since becoming a star to grow her fan base (for our purposes as businesspeople, we can also call them her customer base) provide a model for companies, brands, and nonprofits to emulate. A lot of Lady Gaga's marketing intuition comes from putting varied and dramatic life experiences to use, and those experiences can give us a lens through which to study what she does well and how she does it. Many marketers would kill to have Lady Gaga as their "product" to sell versus having to sell toilet paper or laundry detergent. Her catchy songs, crazy stage performances, and wacky outfits make her quite unique and buzz worthy. But I believe it is Lady Gaga's ability to remain singularly focused on maintaining her fan base that has made her as successful as she is today. This is what sets her apart from the traditional way of doing business and where traditional businesses can learn the most from her success. This chapter will focus on Lady Gaga's biography and background as the first step toward understanding how she built an extremely successful music career using intuitive marketing strategies that businesses can learn to emulate.

Gaga was born Stefani Joanne Angelina Germanotta on March 28, 1986. She grew up in New York City, raised by Italian American parents Joe and Cynthia. Stefani was a musical prodigy. She began playing the piano at the age of four, wrote her first piano ballad at thirteen, and started to perform at open-mike nights when she was fourteen. At age seventeen, she was accepted into the prestigious Collaborative Arts Project 21, a musical theater–training conservatory at New York University's Tisch School of the Arts, which shows that other people understood her talent as well. She explained to *The Telegraph* (London) why her classical training was an important background for a pop songwriter, saying, "I was classically trained as a pianist and that innately teaches you how to write a pop song, because when you learn Bach inversions, it has the same sort of modulations between the chords. It's all about tension and release. But I want to do something that speaks to everyone. To me there is nothing more powerful than one song that you can put on in a room anywhere in the world and somebody gets up and dances." Her status as a prodigy and her history as a classically trained pianist are, in some ways, the first steps toward her success. She had the goods and her talent makes her longevity as a music icon more likely because fans don't stay loyal to someone who doesn't embody a meaningful, quality experience.

Gaga's discerning, hard-core fans have always been able to separate her talent from the costumes and over-the-top performances. An appearance on Howard Stern's SiriusXM radio show on July 18, 2011, gives a window into how people respond to her talent and how she converts them into fans. After an in-depth ninety-minute interview, covering a variety of topics, Gaga performed two songs. She accompanied herself on piano and belted out a soaring acoustic rendition of "The Edge of Glory" that Stern remarked was "one of the best performances we've ever had on the show." Reaction from her non-fans, based on remarks made online, was that it was the stripped-down performances that turned them into Gaga converts. "Wow. Helluva set of pipes. That performance wiped away most of my snark re: Gaga." There was a similar reaction when Gaga, while on tour in Japan, sat in with a band at the bar at the Tokyo Park Hyatt. She played piano and belted out a jazzy rendition of the 1950s classic "Orange Colored Sky." On a YouTube video captured by someone in the audience, you can hear a man shout over the music to his companion "I love her now! I didn't like her before, but now I do." Her talent speaks for itself and is, in large part, why people respect and admire her. Gaga with just a piano has the power to change people's minds about her.

There is an important lesson here: It is very difficult, if not impossible, to build loyalty around a subpar product. If a product is defective, there is going to be negative word of mouth. With an average product, there is usually very little word of mouth. There is nothing to talk about. In order to captivate customers, the brand/product/company/nonprofit must be remarkable in the most literal sense. That is, there must be something about it that is worth remarking on. Gaga is the perfect example of this. But when people just see over-the-top outfits and weird hair, Gaga evangelists can pull out the videos of her singing acoustically and show that she has the goods. And these evangelists—these core fans or customers—remain loyal over time and bring others into the fold.

Before she became a star, however, Stefani took many detours. To the dismay of her parents, she withdrew from Tisch to focus on her music career. Her father, Joe, agreed to pay her rent for one year on the condition that she reenroll if she was unsuccessful. "I left my entire family, got the cheapest apartment I could find, and ate shit until somebody would listen," she told *New York* magazine. This is the first real risk she took and it began an experimental phase in Gaga's life that would ultimately influence her onstage persona. She connected with a music producer, Rob Fusari, who not only helped shape her sound from rock to electronic dance but also accidently played a part in coming up with the "Lady Gaga" moniker after comparing some of her harmonies with those of Freddie Mercury, lead singer of Queen. Gaga was brainstorming stage names when she was texted "Lady Gaga" by Fusari. "Every day, when Stef came to the studio, instead of saying hello, I would start singing [the Queen song] 'Radio Ga Ga.' That was her entrance song. The text message was the result of a predictive text glitch that changed 'radio' to 'lady.' She texted back, 'That's it,' and declared, 'Don't ever call me Stefani again.'" Under the new name, she started writing songs, formed a band, and played small clubs around New York. She attended neo-burlesque shows and began go-go dancing in bars, dressed in a bikini. She also experimented with drugs.

After Gaga met performance artist Colleen Martin, aka Lady Starlight, at a party in Manhattan, they became fast friends, and Gaga began to realize that there was more to a music career than just playing music. Eleven years her senior, Starlight became Gaga's mentor. Starlight taught the aspiring performer how to make over-the-top costumes. "The outfits were quite often stuck together with glue. Sometimes they held up, and sometimes they fell apart on stage. We always wanted the flashiest garments possible . . . and to be as naked as possible," Starlight said. "But I was the one who told her to take her trousers off because I rarely wore any myself." The two performed together as "Lady Gaga and the Starlight Revue" with their show billed as "The Ultimate Pop Burlesque Rockshow." It was a low-fi tribute to 1970s variety acts, which featured Gaga on synth and Starlight spinning beats. In the creation of this show, Gaga seemed to understand on a visceral level that performance is about a total experience, not just a musical product, and that constructing that experience for her audience was an important way to make fans.

During this time, things began to look up. In 2007, Gaga signed a music publishing deal with Sony/ATV and began writing songs for Britney Spears, New Kids on the Block, Fergie, and the Pussycat Dolls. She was still hoping to break out as a star herself, so she began looking to past cultural icons for inspiration. Fascinated with pop culture, she bought books about Andy Warhol, learning about how stardom could be its own art form. She started to develop an awareness of cultural and consumer trends, an awareness that continues to serve her well to this day. "Andy's books became her bible," says Darian Darling, a friend. "She would highlight them with a pen." Gaga told *Seattle Weekly*, "I have a fascination with Andy Warhol and the way he wanted to make commercial art that was taken as seriously as fine art. Music has gotten so pretentious that now it's almost rebellious to be a pop artist. A lot of indie-rock bands and singer-songwriters have this middle finger up at the pop world and record labels." Gaga became a student of pop culture and, with a tenacity not many pop stars or businesses have, she armed herself with an understanding of what a culture embraces and why.

It was then that she began a transformation, and who she wanted to be as a musician and a performer came together. She came up with a persona—a product, so to speak—and hit upon her first incarnation as a star. She collaborated with a little-known Moroccan producer who went by the name RedOne and specialized in electronic music and synthpop. Together, they wrote a club song called "Just Dance." She dyed her brunette hair blond. She started wearing metallic, space age–inspired outfits. For performances, she sported a lightning bolt appliqué over one eye, channeling David Bowie.

Little did she know, her biggest break was about to happen. One day hip-hop artist and producer Akon was struggling to lay down some tracks for his second album, *Konvicted*. Gaga was asked to come into the studio and sing a reference vocal for Akon. A reference vocal is like a blueprint that the artist follows when laying down the final track. It's used as a reference, then thrown out when the final work is done. Akon was so blown away by Gaga's singing that he signed her to his Kon Live record label and started working with her on her first EP,

*The Fame.* The album dealt with Gaga's fascination with fame and was released in August 2008 with the first four singles, "Just Dance," "Poker Face," "Love Game," and "Paparazzi," all shooting to No. 1 on the *Billboard* chart. *The Fame Monster*, her sophomore effort, was released in November 2009. Each song on the album related, from personal experience, to the darker side of fame and is expressed through a monster metaphor. The first two singles from the album, "Bad Romance" and "Telephone," both went to No. 1. In fact, Gaga was the first artist in history to have her first six singles all go to No. 1 on the *Billboard* pop chart. She performed for 2.4 million people in 202 shows in twenty-eight countries on the year-and-a-half-long Monster Ball Tour. Her popularity skyrocketed in a very short period of time and culminated with *Rolling Stone* naming her the current Queen of Pop. As we talk about in business, it was her hockey-stick moment—the point in time when all the data points that have been humming along horizontally suddenly shoot vertical. Her time had come.

It's important to understand Gaga's background and how she went from Stefani to the world's top pop star because much of her childhood and life experiences in New York have shaped who she is today. Her biography continues to influence how she approaches her fan (or customer) base in a way that most musicians, bands, and businesses don't. It's important to study what she does, how she does it, and why, because there are ways to replicate her success in more traditional business settings. I believe it is Gaga's tremendous intuition and her desire to create meaningful relationships with her fans that guide her in all things related to Little Monsters. In the next seven chapters, I am going to dissect what she is doing and present it in a way that businesses and nonprofits can learn from. Gaga's business of show business may be very different from your type of business, but her focus on growing through devoted customer loyalty is a universal business objective. In the next chapter, we will look into her unique fan philosophy of focusing most of her efforts on a very small part of her fan base—the One Percenters.

# Focus on Your One Percenters

"I'm not the beginning anymore. I don't really see myself anymore as the center. They're the center. I'm the atmosphere around it . . . I will continue to become whatever it is [the fans] would like for me to be."

— **Lady Gaga**

**S**hiny New Object syndrome. It's hard not to get sucked in. We, as businesspeople, are often focused on the newness of things. We are fascinated with the latest and the greatest, and this often distorts our business priorities. Many businesses are consumed with chasing new customers instead of focusing on the ones that they have. We see this all the time with companies who will give heavily discounted offers to new customers to get them in the door while longtime customers are left wondering why their loyalty isn't being rewarded with the same offers.

A 2011 study by Forrester Research and Heidrick & Struggles shows the obsession of chief marketing officers who are focused on the "new" factor: new customers, new products, new awareness (see Fig. 1.1). CMOs were asked to name their current top three marketing objectives.

Fifty-nine percent of CMOs say acquiring new customers is one of their top priorities. What about current customers? Only 30 percent of CMO respondents say they are focused on retaining customers as a top priority. Just over a quarter of respondents, at 26 percent, say better customer lifetime value and customer satisfaction/advocacy is a key objective. This couldn't be more obvious in industries like cable/satellite TV service—

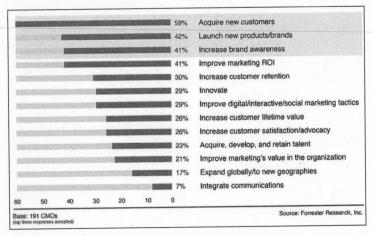

| | |
|---|---|
| 59% | Acquire new customers |
| 42% | Launch new products/brands |
| 41% | Increase brand awareness |
| 41% | Improve marketing ROI |
| 30% | Increase customer retention |
| 29% | Innovate |
| 29% | Improve digital/interactive/social marketing tactics |
| 26% | Increase customer lifetime value |
| 26% | Increase customer satisfaction/advocacy |
| 23% | Acquire, develop, and retain talent |
| 21% | Improve marketing's value in the organization |
| 17% | Expand globally/to new geographies |
| 7% | Integrate communications |

60  50  40  30  20  10  0

Base: 191 CMOs
(top three responses accepted)

Source: Forrester Research, Inc.

**Fig. 1.1** An index of the top priorities of Chief Marketing Officers (CMOs). Evidently, CMOs are suffering from Shiny New Object syndrome.

industries focused on acquiring as many new customers as possible at the expense of existing ones. According to a Satmetrix 2012 Net Promoter Benchmark Study of U.S. Consumers, of the twenty-two industries that Satmetrix examined, the cable/satellite TV service industry has one of the worst average scores in current customer satisfaction by far (8 percent), beat out in mediocrity only by health care (4 percent) and Internet services (4 percent), though Internet may be so low because it is often bundled with cable/TV. In the cable/satellite TV industry, customers gripe all the time about lack of customer service for existing customers. One quick scroll of the Yelp page for Time Warner Cable in Austin, Texas, shows just how many customers are upset at how they're treated. Ceee D. says, "Holy sheeit. Look at all of these 1 star reviews. BELIEVE IT. Unfortunately, they are spot on. TWC is ok as long as you are a new customer

& you never need to contact them for any reason. Otherwise, you are in for pure, unadulterated HELL."

This is where companies like these have gotten it wrong. According to the tried and true research from TARP Worldwide, it is five times cheaper to keep a customer than to get a new one. The CMO priorities heavily focused on new customers don't add up. And this focus is often at the expense of existing customers—customers who, if you retained them, would help bring in new customers just on the basis of customer satisfaction and word of mouth.

Where other businesses don't seem to connect, though, Gaga gets the math. It's her overarching philosophy to focus on her core advocates, the superfans, the Little Monsters. These advocates will ultimately be evangelists who bring in new customers on their own. For Gaga, I believe this is an intuitive decision, not driven by numbers alone. Perhaps because of her traditional family upbringing, loyalty is very important to her. She feels that she needs to reward the loyalty of fans who supported her early in her career. You will learn in a later chapter that even after she became the biggest pop star on the planet, she would stop by small clubs that took a chance on her early in her career, when she was in their city. She wanted to reward their loyalty. Also, she is not interested in converting those people who do not understand her. And there are a lot of people who don't. Gaga told *Cosmopolitan* magazine, "I ate (expletive) for so long, being told I didn't fit the mold and that I was 'too pop' or 'too theater' . . . I've always been delusionally ambitious to the point where people don't understand me." But

**Fig. 1.2** Super-engaged customers often make up just 1 percent of the customer base.

her core fans do understand her and those are the fans Gaga concentrates on.

I call these core customers who are super-engaged the One Percenters. This core group of customers, in general, makes up about 1 percent of a business's customer base. (see Fig. 1.2)

This idea of the One Percenters is based on research that my coauthor Ben McConnell and I did for our 2007 book, *Citizen Marketers*. In the early days of online community and social media, we looked at online communities and tracked what percentage of members in those communities created content. In other words, who was most engaged. We found it amounted to just 1 percent of the total community members. Another 10 percent of the community interacted with that content by commenting on it or rating it, and the other 89 percent were just lurkers. This was surprising. The amount of super-engaged community members did not follow the usual 80/20 rule (aka the Pareto principle), which states that 80 percent of value comes from 20 percent of participants. Our research was showing the volume of content creators was much smaller, at just 1 percent. One percent is a very small part of the community, and yet this disproportionate number was creating most of the value for the entire community.

You could call the One Percenters "customer evangelists." In fact, this was the title of my first book—*Creating Customer Evangelists*—and I believe that many of the traits my coauthor and I discovered about these customers apply to the One Percenters. If you observe the following traits in your customer base, they just might be One Percenters:

- **They passionately recommend your company to friends, neighbors, and colleagues.** New customers are made because a friend wouldn't stop talking about a product or service, especially about how it changed her life.

- **They believe in the company and its people.** Customers may actually profess their belief in your mission statement, especially if it is focused on changing the world.

- **They purchase your products and services as gifts.** They want their friends to experience what they love.

- **They provide unsolicited praise or suggestions of improvement.** They have moved beyond simple word of mouth into deep-rooted evangelism by offering you their time and knowledge. They have pressed themselves into volunteerism.

- **They forgive occasional subpar seasons or dips in customer service.** Because they have invested some time in understanding your business, they know the score. They understand the challenges of running a business and that no one is perfect. They have built a relationship with you, and relationships are never perfect.

- **They do not want to be bought.** Creating a paid-referral system for existing customers to recruit new ones is like paying a family member to show up for dinner. You can do it, but it changes the dynamic of the relationship. Paying customer evangelists turns volunteerism into labor.

- **They feel part of something bigger than themselves.** They have connected with your brand or company at an intrinsic, emotional level. They want to meet other like-minded customers who believe in what they believe in. And that's you.

There are a number of businesses, which I'll highlight later on in the book, that have these kinds of One Percenters. MINI and Method are two that come to mind. Gaga, and her manager, Troy Carter, also understand that the secret to long-term success is focusing on the One Percenters. This is quite different from many artists in the music industry. Think of Gaga's pop contemporaries: Nicki Minaj, Rihanna, Katy Perry. All very popular now, but will they be popular ten or twenty years from now? All sing catchy pop tunes. All wear crazy outfits that get people talking. But none of them seem to have much depth behind their personas. Don't get me wrong; they have rabid fans. However, they aren't doing anything to cater to their most loyal fans the way Gaga is. Gaga and Carter are willing to invest now in the customer base that they want years from now. Gaga explained to *The Guardian* in 2009, "I don't wanna be one song. I wanna be the next 25 years of pop music. But it's really hard to measure that kind of ambition. That kind of blonde ambition is looked at with a raised brow, because most artists don't have longevity today, especially in fun music that's about underwear and pornography and money."

Gaga's popularity was meteoric after her first No. 1 song, "Let's Dance." As her notoriety grew, so did the number of followers on Twitter and Facebook. As of this writing, Gaga is the most followed person on Twitter, with more than thirty-three million followers. On Facebook, she is among the top "liked" celebrities, with more than fifty-five million likes. But the super die-hard fans also hang out on the Gaga fan sites that have sprung up. The most popular sites are GagaDaily.com, GagaNews.com, and PropaGaga.com. Not only do the fan sites track Gaga's every move on their blogs but they provide forums where fans can talk with one another. This breeds a real sense of community among the fans who really "get" the eclectic performance artist.

In late 2010, Gaga and her team realized that they could create their own private place for the superfans, the Little Monsters. Gaga herself dreamed up the idea after seeing an advance screening of *The Social Network*, a movie about the rise of Facebook. "Why don't we start one of those for my fans?" she asked her manager. Carter loved the idea. He partnered with some of the best in Silicon Valley, and created a firm called Backplane, which would build a niche social-network platform that could be used by other artists and even brands. Gaga invested her own money in the venture. Gaga's social network is called Littlemonsters.com and it is built completely around the superfans.

In February 2012, a beta version of the site was opened to one thousand influential fans, including the creators of the independent Gaga fan sites. The site looks like a cross between Pinterest and reddit, with a scrolling wall of Gaga fan art and photos submitted by the Little Monsters. Fans can set up a profile, message one another, and find links to concert dates. They even get their own Littlemonsters.com e-mail address, linking their online identity to Gaga. On February 10, 2012, Lady Gaga herself set up a profile and started communicating with fans. Laura Lyne, a journalism student from Dublin, Ireland, who had cofounded the GagaNews.com fan site, was used to interacting with Gaga's management. Carter and Gaga's staff had for years been embracing the fan sites to update them on upcoming news and projects. But Lyne told *Wired* magazine that Little monsters.com takes it to a completely different level. She explains, "Lady Gaga seems to go on on a regular basis. She's updating all the time. There's a love icon, and she's clicking that on things that stand out. A couple of weeks ago, she tweeted some fan art that she found on the site. It was an amazing thing that she would never have seen otherwise. The fans are getting this amazing opportunity. It's what makes it so unique."

So how does the One Percenters formula work for Gaga? It's a little difficult to estimate the size of Gaga's fan base. Measures could include albums sold, singles sold, concert tickets sold, etcetera. But a look at the number of her followers on Facebook or Twitter could be a good clue. There is surely overlap of fans following Gaga on two of the most popular social-media sites. However, if you examine the amount of engagement she has with fans on the two sites—retweets and favorites on her tweets, and "likes" and comments on her Facebook posts—Facebook wins hands down. A recent photo of herself labeled "Chicago fire," a reference to her actor boyfriend's upcoming television show, got 113,000 likes in two hours. Let's use, then, the 55 million likes on Facebook as our total community number. Then the One Percent Rule would dictate that the number of superfans would equal approximately 1 percent of that number, or 550,000. On August 25, 2012, Gaga tweeted the following, "Very excited to tell you that [Littlemonsters.com] is now approaching HALF A MILLION USERS! Our baby is growing up!" The One Percent Rule is holding true for Gaga.

Gaga and her management team took a strategic step to invest in an engagement vehicle for the One Percenters. Carter knows that Littlemonsters.com is a very lucrative asset for his client and has discussed the possibility of someday selling music and other things Gaga-related directly to the superfans. While other artists are still chasing followers on Twitter and Facebook, Carter is unperturbed. He admits that these social sites are good for the raw numbers, but he and Gaga are focused more on their own One Percenters network. Carter says of the fans on Littlemonsters.com, "They're highly motivated fans . . . This one isn't for the passive. It's for the die-hard die-hard. We could go to Facebook for pure numbers. But give us 500,000 really engaged people, and the blast radius will be enormous." Gaga recruits new superfans into the private network by posting all photos, videos, or long letters to fans on Littlemonsters.com first. Then she will post Littlemonsters.com links to the content on Twitter and Facebook. Fans follow the links and this is how they find out about the community.

Nurturing and growing the One Percenters takes dedication and deference to this core customer base. Gaga's commitment to her vision and her fans was tested in 2012 during the Born This Way Ball Tour. Police in the Indonesian capital city of Jakarta would not issue a permit because hard-line Islamic groups threatened violence if Gaga went ahead with her concert stop there. The Islamic Defenders Front (FPI) called Gaga a "devil's messenger in a bra and panties" and claimed her show was too vulgar for citizens. Indonesia is officially secular but has more Muslims than any other country. More than fifty thousand tickets had already sold. Police told Gaga they would issue the venue permit only if she agreed to tone down the show. Gaga and her management said they would rather cancel dates on her tour than make changes to appease censors and religious groups. Carter told the Music Matters Asia Conference in Singapore that fervid opposition was more a rejection of everything that the singer represents than anything to do with her wardrobe or onstage behavior. "I don't think this has anything to do with Gaga as much as it has to do with—you know, it's just a big cultural and generational gap that is happening over there," Carter told the audience. "You are dealing with a few different things, you are dealing with politics . . . you are dealing with religion. It's a little bit more complicated than her changing her outfits." Though she was devastated to cancel the show, Gaga felt she would be letting the Little Monsters down if she didn't stand up for her vision and for them. She didn't want Indonesian fans to get a substantially pared-down show. "We cater to a very, very, very specific audience," Carter said. "This is an audience that we feel we are going to have longevity with. This is the audience that hopefully twenty years from now, Gaga can still play for this audience, as they grow older and as she grows older. So it's very important that she maintains her loyalty and integrity with this audience and hopefully they'll follow her."

The reaction from the Indonesian Little Monsters reflects the loyalty Gaga has shown them. In a show of solidarity and support, ninety-one of Gaga's biggest fans gathered at Jakarta's eX Plaza Indonesia shopping center for a flash-mob tribute to the singer. They were dressed in iconic Gaga-esque costumes and performed a choreographed dance number while surprised shoppers looked on, filming the entire routine on their camera phones. In the ten-minute video uploaded to YouTube, the group dances to a medley of Gaga songs before triumphantly embracing at the performance's end. They used the performance to send a message to the nation's conservative Islamist groups, and to Gaga herself, with a written note at the end of the video: "Tons of rejection and hatred are everywhere. But still, we will always [get] your back. We respect your decision due to BTW Ball cancellation, and it DOESN'T change how much we love you. We love you, Mother Monster, 'til the end."

The outpouring of support moved Gaga, as you can imagine. She posted a link to the video on her Twitter account, along with a response to her Indonesian Monsters. "This made me cry so hard," Gaga wrote. "I love you so much. You are the best fans in the world." It was a moment that bonded the worldwide Little Monster community, with one commenter on the You-Tube video saying, "I love this so much. it's so beautiful how courageous everyone who did this is; to dress like that in such a closed minded country. I have so much pride for my fellow monsters in Indonesia. instead of not doing anything, you said, 'screw it, we're going to have our own concert.' I'm dancing along with you and putting my paws up."

Smart companies are focusing on growing their businesses by engaging the One Percenters. There's no magic potion; it takes patience and a focus on the long term. There may be temptations to take shortcuts and not grow organically. Gaga's manager fought this urge. Even though she could've played bigger venues early in her career because the demand was there, he wanted her to play small venues so that the audience could really connect with her. "One of the biggest things . . . is the discovery process. And making sure that [the] audience feels like they have ownership in it." His advice on growing your One Percenters: "It's about not skipping a step, [but instead] doubling down on whatever audience that has found you."

Gaga wants to be around for a long time to come, so she is doing the smart thing by investing in her One Percenters now. This is a strategic business move, and probably the most important thing other companies and organizations can learn from her. Organically growing a grassroots base of passionate customers who stay loyal and help you build your business will pay dividends over the long term. Once you have adopted this strategy, the next step on the road to engaging the One Percenters is to start with what's meaningful or, as Lesson 2 will show, to lead with values.

# Lead with Values

"It has nothing to do with the way that I dress or how I sound. It has everything to do with the power of the message."

**— Lady Gaga**

An important step in creating passionate, loyal customers is not just to focus on the features and benefits of your product or service but to make sure customers know that your business is about something bigger. By bigger, I mean something emotional that people can believe in. Features and benefits speak to the analytical side of what you are selling. Your values, what your company believes in, and how you are changing customers' lives for the better communicates the emotional side of what you are selling. Customers can be interested in what products do, but they can only bond with companies emotionally over what they believe in. There are different words to describe this set of beliefs: "core values," "purpose," "cause," "ideals," or, as we'll see later in the chapter, Simon Sinek's "the why." Coauthors Richard Cross and Janet Smith call this "identity bonds" that are formed between customer and company. "Identity bonds are formed when customers admire and identify with values, attitudes, or lifestyle preferences that they associate with your brand or product," they write in *Customer Bonding: Pathway to Lasting Customer Loyalty*. "Customers form an emotional attachment based on their perception of those shared values." Whatever you decide to name it, I'm referring to the notion of connecting with customers around something bigger than just the tangible products and services listed on your Web site. In this chapter, we will examine how Lady Gaga epitomizes embracing ideals and how she embodies them. We will examine why it's important for businesses also to lead with values, the business performance of organizations who do, and ultimately how to reorient one's approach to the market to start with "the why."

## The Five Dimensions of a Cause

Guy Kawasaki knows a little something about leading with values. He was one of the first Apple "evangelists," employees who were tasked with selling software developers on the value proposition of building their products on the nascent computer company's hardware. It was an uphill battle for Kawasaki and his compatriots at Apple. They were up against behemoth IBM, thirty-five times bigger, decades older, and embraced by businesspeople. At this time, in 1983, Apple didn't even have a working prototype, so they couldn't compete on features. But they did have a dream to increase the productivity and creativity of people by challenging the status quo. It was Kawasaki's job to be an evangelist for Apple and sell this dream.

Kawasaki shares his experience of making the "sell" about something bigger at Apple in his book, *Selling the Dream*. In the book, he explains that you have to start with your values, or as he calls it, a cause. Kawasaki goes on to explain that causes do five things:

Embody a vision

Make people better

Generate big effects

Catalyze selfless actions

Polarize people

Do your company's values do these five things? Mapping your values against these five dimensions is a good exercise to go through as you refine your core values and beliefs. Let's map Gaga against these five dimensions to explore how she makes her business about something bigger than just selling pop music.

## Embody a vision

A vision is a person or company's perception of how to change the world, even if it is just the part of the world that is important to their customers. Gaga's vision is to transform the culture to create a kinder, braver world where everyone is valued. Her fans embrace her vision, as this example shows:

There are artists that will define a generation. The Beatles, Elvis, Frank Sinatra, Michael Jackson. Their influence is far reaching and extends far beyond their music. And you are one, too.

It's so funny how the mainstream media only will consider you a singer. You are more than just a singer. You are a songwriter, pianist, performance artist, social media pioneer, and social activist. With every breath that you take, you inspire millions.

—Corey Sheeran, Lakewood CA

Perhaps Gaga's road toward her vision began when as a child she was bullied. One particular incident that she has shared occurred in high school. "The boys picked me up and threw me in the trash can on the street, on the corner of my block while all the other girls from the school were leaving and could see me in the trash," she revealed in a MTV special. She tried to hold back the tears.

"Everybody was laughing and I was even laughing. I had that nervous giggle . . . I remember even one of the girls looking at me, like 'Are you about to cry? You're pathetic.' That's what it felt like, 'you're pathetic.'" She admitted being too embarrassed to tell anyone, even her parents, about the incident. Many of her fans can relate to this experience.

Her vision of a kinder, braver world and the value she places on participating in making the world a safer and better place may be traced to incidents like these. Those scars run deep and don't go away. Gaga told Oprah in an interview at her childhood home in New York City:

[For] all the fame and fortune, the praise that you receive, something inside of you is always scarred by those experiences. I work every day to become a more confident human being, as we all do. But there are moments that I wonder if it's true. That is the shame of it all. And that is what I want to help with the most. It seems almost ridiculous that I would be sitting with Oprah Winfrey in my mother's kitchen and saying that sometimes I feel worthless. When you experience the feeling of being picked up and thrown in the trash in public, something like that can really stay with you for life. And it really stayed with me.

And so, Gaga is passionate about her vision, in part because it comes from her own experience and that makes her understand its importance personally. She explained in an interview with *The Advocate* magazine, "I care only about what I can change. What can I push forward? How can I be a part of the fight for modern social issues? How can I change young people's lives? How can I create a show and an album that is a portal to surreality, to free ourselves of all of our insecurities and to be proud of who we are? I'm a fucking hippie in that way, and that's just who I am."

She alludes to creating a kinder, braver world with the symbolism associated with the *Born This Way* album. Her launch of the "Born This Way" single at the 2011 Grammy Awards was a performance in which she was "born" out of an egg-shaped vessel to signify a new race of nonprejudicial, nonjudgmental people. In the video for the song, she more fully explores the "birthing a new race" idea with many "birthing" scenes. I have to say, even I was a bit shocked at the explicitness of these scenes. She went over the top to communicate her vision of a new, braver, kinder world that was being created.

### Make people better

Your values should make people perform or feel better. For example, Apple makes its customers feel more creative and productive. Nonprofits with a societal cause, like Mothers Against Drunk Driving (MADD) whose mission is to lower the rate of drunk driving in the United States, attempt to make the world a safer place for us all. Gaga makes people better by inspiring them to be brave, and to be the best people they can be. She wants her fans to love themselves and not worry about what haters think of them. And you can see the effects of her inspiration in letters like this one:

Dear Mama Monster,

I'm proud to say that you've helped me so much. Through the darkest of times, you've helped me see the light.

I have become a much more compassionate and stronger person because of you. I can honestly say I've become a better person. Whenever I get bullied or teased, it doesn't affect me because of what you have taught your Little Monsters. I'm no longer the insecure girl I used to be.

Whenever I see an injustice, I try to stop it because I know it would make you proud. Whenever I'm in a tough situation, I always say to myself, "What would Gaga do?" because that will ALWAYS be the best way to go about something . . .

> — Love and Paws Up, Your Little Monster
> Liza, Minnesota

This is just one of thousands of fan letters you can find on the Web, especially on Tumblr. At the time of this writing, a Google search for "Gaga changed my life" turned up 3,880,000 results. The search results highlight heartfelt Tumblr posts, blog posts, tweets, videos, and posts on Littlemonsters.com from fans telling Gaga how she has made their lives better. Many of the fans talk about feeling bad about themselves and being inspired by Gaga's music and her message as well as the way she lives her life. Because she was bullied, some feel a connection to her because it happened to them, too. They feel she is one of them. "The fans lead the music. And it just so happens that a lot of my fans have shared with me their stories," Gaga has said.

> I traveled all over the world, and every night when the show was over, I would stop outside the arena and take pictures and sign autographs. And sometimes when it was really cold out, I would invite 30 fans on the bus and give them hot chocolate, give them Cheetos. Ask them if they were okay and they would say, "My dad kicked me out because I'm gay." I would meet fans who were beat up outside of school or had to move high schools be-

cause they were teased for being fat. I can go on and on about the stories. But it wasn't until they shared their stories with me that I realized how like them I was, and I began to relive all of my struggles as a teenager.

So for one of them to overcome her obstacles and become the biggest pop star in the world gives them hope. I'm amazed at how emotional and personal the connection is with the fans, given that they have never met this woman. I believe this has to do with her transparency and accessibility to her fans. This is a great lesson for businesses, especially large ones, that hope to create emotional bonds with their customers. Transparency and accessibility are key in helping customers understand how you are trying to make their lives better.

### Generate big effects

Your values should scale. That is, they should affect a lot of people. Or they could affect relatively few people, but still the majority of a smaller group. For Gaga, this means taking a stand to help not just her fans, but kids just like her fans, who have been bullied and lack self-confidence. "It's about society, but it's also about pledging a certain allegiance to your fan base," she explained in an interview with the *Huffington Post*. "It's not like, 'Thanks for buying my record, f*ck you'; it's like, 'Thanks for buying my record—and I will live and die and breathe my work and my art to protect your dreams. Because you protect mine.'"

In November 2011, Gaga announced that she was starting a nonprofit called the Born This Way Foundation, the mission of which is to empower youth by offering mentoring and career development, and focusing on issues like self-confidence, well-being, and anti-bullying. The Born This Way Foundation was established in partnership with Harvard University, the California Endowment, and the MacArthur Foundation. She appointed her mother, Cynthia Germanotta, as president. Gaga had called the foundation a passion project for her and her mother, saying, "Together we hope to establish a standard of Bravery and Kindness, as well as a community worldwide that protects and nurtures others in the face of bullying and abandonment."

Although Gaga has not said so publicly, her passion to do something big and launch a foundation may be due to one particular fan, Jamey Rodemeyer. Rodemeyer, a passionate Gaga fan, was an openly gay fourteen-year-old from Buffalo, New York, who was known for his YouTube activism against homophobia. Rodemeyer's inspiration to help others came from Gaga and he often referred to her in his videos and quoted her lyrics to provide guidance to others. He even made a video for the It Gets Better Project, a nonprofit organization with a Web site dedicated to preventing teen suicide, saying that Lady Gaga always made him happy, letting him know that he was "born this way." Ultimately unable to escape incessant bullying, Jamey took his own life in September 2011. His last Twitter message was to his idol: "@ladygaga bye mother monster, thank you for all you have done, paws up forever." Gaga was devastated by the news, tweeting about Jamey and saying, "The past days I've spent reflecting, crying, and yelling." She continued, "I have so much anger. It is hard to feel love when cruelty takes someone's life." She promised fans that she would fight for hate-crime laws against bullying and meet with President Obama on the matter. She kept her promise and addressed the president on the issue at a private event later that month. She studied the problem of bullying and how to eradicate it. She began to realize that no law would really change how people behave. She would have to try to change the culture. No big whoop for a woman who *Time* deemed one of the most influential people in the world.

The Born This Way Foundation was launched at Harvard University in February 2012. Gaga recruited notables such as Oprah Winfrey, Deepak Chopra, and Kathleen Sebelius, secretary of health and human services for the Obama administration, to speak at the launch. Gaga also asked Jamey Rodemeyer's sister, Alyssa, to speak. "This is the beginning of a new movement. . . . This is like Mothers Against Drunk Driving, it's like the antismoking movement, raising consciousness so people get to see that 'enough is enough,'" Oprah said before the event. Deepak Chopra, a friend of Gaga, said of the foundation, "Lady Gaga has used her celebrity and her status as an entertainer to create Little Monsters and her profound program against bullying. I've been an adviser on her foundation and have seen how she's been able to positively impact millions of people on her social networks. She has a unique ability to make people feel that it's okay to be different." Gaga spoke to the overflow crowd, which included local high school and college student volunteers for the foundation, telling them that change starts at the bottom, with them. "What this is all about is saying the power is in your hands," she said. "How can we come together with the greatest experts in the world—you—and come up with all of the amazing ways we can inject love, acceptance, and tolerance into the culture?" She continued, "I'm not here today to give you an answer. The culture of love is not going to change overnight. So we have to start it slowly. But you are the answer. You are the future."

When asked by a panelist about the momentous task of culture change and how long Gaga expected it to take her foundation to show real results, she answered, "It could be 50 years. If I'm dead, I don't give a shit. I just want it to happen."

### Catalyze selfless actions

Powerful causes make even ordinary people do special things. People volunteer, rally others, and go out of their way to share the cause with everyone they know. For businesses, this dimension plays itself out in the passion with which customers willingly recommend their products and services to friends and colleagues. Customers become evangelists, extolling the virtue of a product or company that has changed their lives for the better. For Gaga, her army of Little Monsters is inspired to change the world with her.

One such Little Monster is seventeen-year-old Jacques St. Pierre. St. Pierre is the student council president of Etobicoke School of the Arts in Toronto, Canada, and says he ran for student council president on a platform of equality, anti-bullying, and spreading the message that everybody should be loved and accepted no matter what or who they are. St. Pierre had been bullied for years in elementary school and wanted to do something about it. "I got called the gay kid, the fag, because I liked to be in the school plays," he told the Canadian Broadcasting Company. "I lost my best friend because he joined in with the bullies. It's not fun, I've been there, I've been bullied. Before that, I didn't know bullying could affect people so severely." St. Pierre organized a school assembly with an anti-bullying theme, and he also gathered pledges from fellow students, calling on them to agree to help combat the problem. He also e-mailed dozens of celebrities, asking for help in any way they could. Most e-mails went unanswered. Except the one to Gaga.

"The subject line said 'To Jacques from Lady Gaga,'" St. Pierre explained. "It said 'click on the link below to download the video for your assembly.' So no questions asked, Lady Gaga sent us a video. I watched it, and I started crying. I'm a huge fan. It's kind of embarrassing because I love her so much. I couldn't believe it." In the video Lady Gaga praised St. Pierre for his work to combat bullying, particularly bullying directed at gay and lesbian students. "I just wanted to tell you how proud I am of you for being such a strong advocate of the LGBT community in your school," she said in the video. "There should be more Little Monsters like you." She added, "My father always saves all the fan letters that I receive and I read yours and wanted to send this video to you. It is important that we push the boundaries of love and acceptance."

St. Pierre's classmates were moved by the powerful message of the assembly. "I'm starting to actually realize how big this problem is and I just want to make a difference now," said one male student. Another student said, "I love Lady Gaga and it means so much to me that she could do that for us and support us through this." St. Pierre said he was elated to receive such high-profile support. "Young or old, people know who Lady Gaga is, because she's such a character and she does so much to stand up against bullying in any way she can. And someone as inspiring as her, taking 20 minutes out of her day to write down a speech, sit in front of a teleprompter, get all made up, and read it to us directly at our school. It's fantastic."

Catalyzing selfless actions means those who are inspired by the cause amplify the message through their deeds. Don't be surprised at the amount of things customers will do on your behalf if they believe in your cause.

### Polarize people

Causes that challenge the norm can generate strong feelings. People either love them or hate them. This is a good test for your cause. Does anyone care? Is anyone moved to action? With the good comes the bad. Especially in the Wild West that is YouTube comments. People can be ruthless in social media for things they do not agree with. Gaga believes in the adage "If you're not pissing somebody off, you're not doing your job." She's not afraid to stand up for what she believes in, even if some people vehemently disagree.

Gaga told Oprah, in an interview about the positive and negative response to the "Born This Way" message,

> You know how you know you hit the nerve? Because everyone doesn't wave a flag that says "I love Gaga." You got a bunch of "I love her," you got a bunch of "I hate her." And "I don't get it" and "what is this rubbish" and "explain it to me." And I said, This is it. I hit the nerve . . . you have to hit the nerve . . . it's like a volcano. It can't erupt unless something goes haywire. It has to emerge. It has to explode. I'm not interested in making lukewarm pop music or lukewarm philanthropic efforts. I'm not interested in just raising money and throwing it against the wall for an organization that I don't even know about. What I want to do is strike your nerve over and over and over again to get you talking so that you can be a part of this message that will change everything.

Gaga has been the subject of protests in her career, especially among extremist religious groups. As I mentioned earlier, Islamic extremists in Jakarta, Indonesia, threatened violence if she went ahead with her concert in the city. Christian youths in the Philippines protested Gaga's concert tours, saying that they were offended by her music, particularly the song "Judas," which they said mocks Jesus Christ. Christian groups in South Korea also protested her concerts, claiming her songs promote homosexuality and pornography. A U.S.-based organization called the Florida Family Association (FFA), which aims to "educate people on what they can do to defend, protect and promote traditional, biblical values," decried the partnership between the Born This Way Foundation and Office Depot. The organization was upset that Office Depot was selling a line of back-to-school items with the Foundation's messages on them and donating 25 percent of the sales with a guaranteed $1 million donation to the Foundation. Apparently the FFA was afraid that the products, including Post-it notes emblazoned with messages like "Be yourself," would "influence many teens to embrace homosexuality for their lifetime who may have otherwise worked through their crisis with straight results." Neither Office Depot nor Gaga formally responded to these comments.

Gaga doesn't back down to protests and has learned to take the haters in stride. When a fan thanked Gaga via Twitter for helping her deal with bullies, Gaga tweeted back, "its [sic] easier than you think. I go through people saying bad things about me, sometimes publicly. Feel empathy for their anger." She's told fans on the Born This Way Ball Tour that she's recently learned a lot about negativity and people trying to tear you down. She says she doesn't want to fight back because it's more important to focus on her fans and writing music. The lesson here is that when you try to change the status quo or the industry norm, some people will not like it. These people cannot be converted. Don't waste time and energy on them. Instead, focus on your cause, what you produce, and your customers.

Meaningful experiences and interactions are what we all long for and seek out. The most successful companies understand this and have found ways to maintain an awareness of the meaning in what they do and to ensure that meaning is conveyed through their products, services, and relationships with customers; it is actually an integral part of what they do and sell.

Now that we know the five dimensions of a cause, we can take a more in-depth look at why it's important to focus on your core beliefs in all that you do.

## Why It's Important to Start with WHY

Author Simon Sinek does a terrific job explaining why some leaders and companies form emotional bonds with customers (or in Lady Gaga's case, fans) and why some don't. In his book, *Start with Why: How Great Leaders Inspire Everyone to Take Action*, Sinek uses a model called the Golden Circle to explain his theory. Here's how he defines the circle's three layers (see Fig. 2.1):

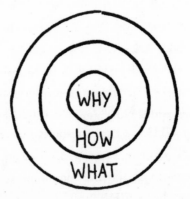

**Fig. 2.1** Simon Sinek's Golden Circle model

**WHAT:** Every single company and organization on the planet knows WHAT they do. This is true no matter how big or small, no matter what industry. Everyone is easily able to describe the products or services a company sells or the job function they have within that system. WHATs are easy to identify.

**HOW:** Some companies and people know HOW they do WHAT they do. Whether you call them a "differentiating value proposition," "proprietary process," or "unique selling proposition," HOWs are often given to explain how something is different or better.

**WHY:** Very few people or companies can clearly articulate WHY they do WHAT they do. When I say WHY, I don't mean to make money—that's a result. By WHY, I mean, what is your purpose, cause, or belief? WHY does your company exist? WHY do you get out of bed every morning? And WHY should anyone care?

Most companies think, act and, communicate from the outside in, from WHAT to WHY. This is the easiest to do—to go from the clearest thing to the fuzziest thing. Sinek concludes, "Usually we say WHAT we do, we sometimes say HOW we do it, but we rarely say WHY we do WHAT we do. Inspiring leaders and companies think, act, and communicate from the inside out. They start with the WHY."

Sinek explains the differences between the two orientations by applying the Golden Circle to a hypothetical marketing message from Apple. I've made a table using his key ideas to serve our purposes here (see Fig. 2.2):

| Outside-in: Starting with WHAT | Inside-out: Starting with WHY |
|---|---|
| • We make great computers.<br>• They're beautifully designed, simple to use, and user-friendly.<br>• Wanna buy one? | • Everything we do, we believe in challenging the status quo.<br>• We believe in thinking differently. The way we challenge the status quo is by making our products beautifully designed, simple to use, and user-friendly.<br>• And we happen to make great computers.<br>• Wanna buy one? |

**Fig 2.2** Hypothetical marketing message from Apple.

Compare these two approaches. They feel different, don't they? Which approach makes you more likely to buy a computer from Apple? The outside-in approach is the one most companies take. This approach attempts to build a rational argument for why their company or product is better than their competitors'. But Apple is not like most companies. From the start, Steve Jobs was a passionate leader who believed in challenging the status quo, and he imbued Apple with its WHY. Apple's ability to create beautiful industry-changing products stems directly from the WHY. By challenging the status quo,

Jobs employed designers and engineers who "think different" and created products that didn't look like or function like the other computers in the industry.

The bottom line: People don't buy WHAT you do, they buy WHY you do it.

That's why we need to start with the WHY. The WHY is bigger than WHAT we are selling. The WHAT is appealing to the rational, analytical side of the brain. The WHY is appealing to the sometimes irrational part of the brain that deals with feelings and loyalty. It's this part of the brain that makes decisions, including decisions on what product to buy or organization to do business with. It's why we have to win not just customers' minds but their hearts as well. Most companies are pretty good at winning minds; that just requires a comparison of product features and benefits. Winning hearts, however, takes more work.

So if we apply Sinek's Golden Circle to Gaga, it would look like this (see Fig. 2.3):

**Fig 2.3** Gaga's WHY–HOW–WHAT.

| Golden Circle Elements | Gaga's Golden Circle |
|---|---|
| WHY | Transform the culture to create a kinder, braver world where everyone is valued. |
| HOW | Live life as performance art, including avant-garde fashion and iconic performances, to gain attention to the cause |
| WHAT | Write and sing catchy pop music |

### The ROI of starting with why

Having an inspirational WHY at the center of your company doesn't just feel good; it also makes good business sense. If your CEO is skeptical about why you want to focus on your WHY, show her the following research from a world-class marketer. A study done by Jim Stengel, former global marketing officer for Procter & Gamble, and Millward Brown Optimor, a global marketing research firm, illustrates the return on investment of starting with WHY, though they use the word "ideals" instead. Stengel and Millward Brown identified and analyzed the fifty fastest-growing brands from 2000 to 2010 in terms of value and consumer preference. They even collaborated with Millward Brown's neuroscience unit to do implicit association testing to measure how quickly people associated words with brands. Their research, which initially involved fifty thousand companies from around the world, showed that people more quickly associated the Stengel 50 (the top fifty businesses in the ten-year-growth study) with their ideals—or purpose—than they did others. The study's results were striking: Companies that were centered on the ideals of improving people's lives outperformed the market by a huge margin. "When we probed to that level . . . we again and again found that the world's fastest-growing enterprises were organized around ideals of improving people's lives and activated these ideals throughout their business ecosystems," says Stengel. The study showed that investment in the Stengel 50 would have been 400 percent more profitable than an investment in the Standard & Poor's (S&P) 500 (see Fig. 2.4.)

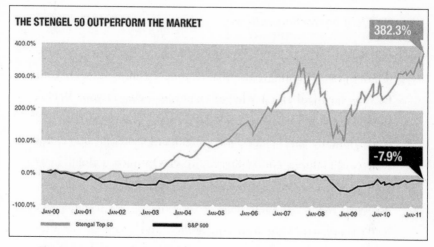

THE STENGEL 50 OUTPERFORM THE MARKET

382.3%

-7.9%

Stengel Top 50          S&P 500

**Fig. 2.4** Companies that lead with values outperform the market.

"The counterintuitive fact is that doing the right thing in your business is doing the right thing for your business. Those that embrace that fact are the ones that dominate their categories, create new categories, and maximize profit in the long term," says Stengel. The Stengel 50 includes companies such as Amazon, Apple, Chipotle, Discovery Communications, Innocent, L'Occitane, Method, Red Bull, Seventh Generation, Stoneyfield Farm, and Zappos. In his book, *Grow: How Ideals Power Growth and Profit at the World's Greatest Companies,* Stengel outlines the "ideals" of each, as he and Millward Brown perceive them. Check out Stengel's book and his complete list of fifty, and see how many brands you connect with. Focusing on one's WHY might seem fuzzy as first, but the math works out. For our purposes in this chapter we'll take a look next at two great examples of businesses that focus on the WHY first: Whole Foods and Method.

## Business example: Whole Foods Market

Whole Foods Market has prospered as a company because it built a business on the belief that people are going to live healthier, happier lives if they eat natural and organic foods. This is their WHY. Whole Foods' founder and CEO John Mackey believes that "businesses that are more conscious of making a positive difference in the world make the world a better place from just being there." He calls this concept of for-profit businesses that lead with values and a higher purpose "conscious capitalism." His theory underscores the importance of all of a company's interdependent "stakeholders": employees, customers, shareholders, suppliers, community, and the environment. When all of those constituencies' interests are factored into the company's decisions and aligned, all—including, not incidentally, the bottom line—will flourish. By any measure, Whole Foods, despite recessionary ups and downs, has flourished. From its humble beginnings in 1980 as a small natural-foods store in Austin, Texas, Mackey has built the grocery chain into a behemoth, with annual revenue of $10.1 billion, 331 locations worldwide and 64,200 employees. It's ranked No. 264 on the Fortune 500.

Whole Foods's motto—"Whole Foods, Whole People, Whole Planet"—emphasizes a vision that reaches far beyond just being a food retailer. The company shares the message behind the motto in every annual report by including the following on the second page of the document:

OUR STAKEHOLDER PHILOSOPHY:

Our "bottom line" ultimately depends on our ability to satisfy all of our stakeholders. Our goal is to balance the needs and desires of our customers, Team Members, shareholders, suppliers, communities, and the environment while creating value for all. By growing the collective pie, we create larger slices for all of our stakeholders. Our core values reflect this sense of collective fate and are the soul of our company.

OUR CORE VALUES:

Selling the **Highest Quality** Natural and Organic Products Available

Satisfying and Delighting Our Customers

Supporting Team Member **Happiness** and **Excellence**

Creating **Wealth** through Profits and Growth

Caring about Our **Communities** and Our Environment

Creating Ongoing **Win-Win Partnerships** with Our Suppliers

Promoting the Health of Our Stakeholders through **Healthy Eating Education**

Whole Foods co-CEO Walter Robb, in an interview with Bonnie Azab Powell, a food, business, and technology reporter, explains the company's focus on leading with values: "Look, we started when this was really small, and it was started from a place of believing that you can make a difference in the world. This retailing comes from our soul. It comes from a desire to effect change in the world. Nothing less than that. Not the money, not the prestige, it comes from a desire to make a difference in the world. From the sense of mission."

When prodded by Powell with "You wrote in a recent article that 'We're not retailers with a mission, we're missionaries who retail.' Explain the difference," Robb responded:

> The deepest core of Whole Foods—the heartbeat, if you will—is this mission of the stakeholder philosophy. If I put it in simple terms it would be, one, to change the way the world eats, and two, to create a workplace based on love and respect. . . . Some people think about this as, "We're going to do our business, and then we'll have a corporate responsibility department." What it really should mean is that you're functioning in a responsible manner that's not outside of your normal functioning, but that you've brought it in as part of who you are and your day-to-day functioning as a company.

It is holding beliefs like this at the core of the company's philosophy that has made Whole Foods successful in terms of profit and effecting positive change in the world. Since 2007, Whole Foods has been on the Ethisphere Institute's World's Most Ethical Companies list as one of only three U.S. companies in the retail-food category on that list. The methodology for the WME ranking includes reviewing codes of ethics and litigation and regulatory infraction histories, evaluating the investment in innovation and sustainable business practices, looking at activities designed to improve corporate citizenship, and studying nominations from senior executives, industry peers, suppliers, and customers. This WME ranking shows that Whole Foods is recognized for embracing the WHY. Whole Foods's core values are at the center of its business philosophy and that is an integral part of its success.

Customers don't just love what Whole Foods sells; they connect with WHY the company sells what it does. A customer comment on Epinions.com recommends others shop at Whole Foods by saying:

> Before I go into detail, let me say that you can find almost anything in Whole Foods that you can find at your supermarket. However, you won't recognize ninety-five percent of the brand names unless you're already a high-end grocery shopper. So why would a person pay higher prices for brands they've never heard of? For me, it's Whole Foods' list of unacceptable ingredients. When you shop at this store, you are not going to get any of [the unacceptable ingredients] in your food. I'm not a doctor, not a nutritionist, etc. I just feel better knowing that these things aren't in my dinner.

## Business example: Method

Method, the green-cleaning products company, offers another chance to look at a company that led with values from the day it was started. According to Method's Facebook page,

Method was founded in 2000—incidentally, in the dirtiest apartment in San Francisco—by Adam Lowry and Eric Ryan, its proud brain-parents and the very first people against dirty™ ... We're in business to change business. Our challenge is to make sure that every product we send out into the world is a little agent of environmental change, using safe and sustainable materials, manufactured responsibly. And that also means no animal testing. When it comes down to it, we're here to make products that work, for you and for the planet.

And Method's WHY isn't just about helping the world through green cleaning. It's also about how artistic design and a focus on beauty can help convince more people to buy eco-friendly products—people who wouldn't normally do so because they don't immediately count that as a value and may think "eco-friendly" implies the product won't work as well as one that uses harsh, toxic chemicals.

Lynn Dornblaser, who tracks consumer product trends at global research house Mintel, says "Method changed consumers' viewpoint from 'this [cleaning product] is something necessary and not good-looking' to 'this is something that's almost an art object that I want everyone who walks into my house to see.' They've lured shoppers who hadn't thought about environmental cleaners by getting them to come in through the back door." Method's products and packaging, originally designed by award-winning, acclaimed industrial designer Karim

Rashid and now designed in-house, are in stores everywhere, including Whole Foods, Staples, Target, and Duane Reade.

Method began its business with the WHY and then moved to the HOW and WHAT. The desire to create something human-friendly and planet-friendly is what motivated them, and this motivation has connected emotionally with customers. This connection continues to be successful for Method, even as customers wavered, during the recession, about buying green products. According to an April 2011 *New York Times* article titled, "As Consumers Cut Spending, 'Green' Products Lose Allure," sales of green cleaning products from big brands like Clorox and S. C. Johnson have dropped precipitously over the past few years. Stephen Powers, an analyst who studies the category at Sanford C. Bernstein & Company, explains, "You see disproportionately negative impact from products like [Clorox] Green Works, out of the big blue-chip companies that have tried to layer a green offering on top of their conventional offering, and a relatively better performance from the niche players who remain independent." Powers went on to say that "sales held up at smaller, and more expensive, brands like Method and Seventh Generation because those customers tended to be more affluent and more wedded to environmental causes." Method reported double-digit growth in 2010 after a flat year in 2009. Big consumer-products companies copied the WHAT, to use Sinek's model. But they weren't credibly leading with the value of changing the world for the better, and they didn't copy Method's HOW of using sleek design to attract customers to their packaging.

Method's cofounder Eric Ryan explained his side of the issue. "It's not that clean products are failing by any means . . . it's that the players that have gone into the green space are not doing it in an authentic way," he says. He acknowledges that the big brands like Clorox Green Works and Arm & Hammer Essentials "did help grow the eco-friendly cleaning product category through low prices, [but if] these companies want to bring in repeat customers, they have to convince them that it's more than just branding—and they can do that by making customers care about what they're buying."

One such customer is Taylor, a "mom" blogger. In her blog *Stain Removal 101*, she says,

> I myself have been tempted to buy Method products before, when I saw them on the shelf, just because they are so bright and colorful, and pretty . . . I actually learned, recently, that the colors that Method uses for its cleaning supplies are all environmentally friendly, too. They want the design and aesthetics of the products to draw people in, and to help them enjoy using the products, but they still keep in mind their overriding mission of green cleaning. Cool, huh? I know that impressed me.

It is no mistake that companies like Method continue to succeed while other companies in the same industry falter. Commitment to a cause and an idea that is bigger than what they are selling motivates and inspires owners and employees to keep finding innovative ways to convince people that their products represent not just something to buy, but a cause worth investing in. In his book *Grow*, Stengel says:

> The ideal—the higher-order benefit the business gives to the world—is rooted in its heritage, which begins with the business's initial reason for being, its founding vision for actively improving the quality of people's lives, and is continuously added to over time. When co-founders Eric Ryan and Adam Lowry started their business, they were very clear that their objective wasn't to create a product or service but to bring to life a transformational ideal. They wanted to articulate an ideal that people could rally around.

And as Eric Ryan tells Stengel, "As human beings, we all want to be part of something bigger than who we are and what we are. When you articulate an ideal and create a cause, it gives people, including myself, the ability to do so much more . . . Everyone—founders, employees, partners we work with, consumers—finds it motivating that there's this common ideal and common mission."

||||||||||||||||||

As with Lady Gaga, Whole Foods and Method aren't just selling merchandise, they're not just selling products, and they're not simply creating a brand. They are figuring out how to turn what they are passionate about and what they believe in into something that others will be passionate about in order to convince others to believe in it, too. They understand that if they are simply trying to sell something for the sake of selling, solely for the sake of making a profit, that they will not convince people for very long. They might get people to try their products once, but they won't create a passion in people to pass the word along. And they won't have lifelong customers or fans. When you start with the WHY, you start with an idea so powerful that convincing customers to believe in it is a much easier thing to do. In the next chapter we will look at how to take the customers that you have convinced of the value inherent in your business and build a community of evangelists.

# Build Community

"The instrument that I never learned how to play was my fans. You know, they are the part of the story that nobody teaches you. I just want to do the right thing; I want to be a voice with them, among them."

— **Lady Gaga**

Gaga doesn't see her fans as walking wallets—customers who merely buy albums and concert tickets and merchandise. She knows her fans make her a success and so she takes her relationship with them very seriously. She knows it is it important to make sure every fan experience is meaningful and memorable, both as a way to maintain fans and as a way to cultivate relationships with potential new ones. When those who aren't yet Little Monsters see how she relates to those who are, they are more likely to desire that meaningful connection as well. As you can see by her letter below, Anja, a die-hard Gaga fan, relies on the Little Monsters community to help her navigate the world and not be so alone, and feels a very powerful connection to other Gaga fans.

> Ever since that first time of you calling out to [your] fans
> as Little Monsters you connected us with a special bond.
> We reached the awareness that there's always someone
> somewhere for us. This way whenever I'm feeling down,
> I have someone to talk to, someone who I have similar
> interests with and thank God for that—who knows what

would happen to me if I had to deal with all the shit that world gives me by myself.

— Anja, 15, Slovenia

Building community starts with finding a common thread that brings people together. Common experiences that the members of a community have had help define what a community is all about and make it possible for members to rely on one another for support. Companies who want to build these kinds of communities have to act small even if they aren't. They need to treat customers like peers and create a feeling of intimacy—a feeling that those customers are part of a group of like-minded people, not merely purchasers to be mass-messaged at. Customers want to converse with companies in a two-way dialogue, and that communication means a lot more when it comes from a peer in the community, someone who is trusted, credible, and easy to relate to. Companies must embrace and continually engage the community of supporters already out there if they want to stay relevant. Gaga is a master at just such community building. There are five key ways she does this:

Connect with like-minded people

Be authentic

Create a collective experience

Celebrate milestones

Encourage collaboration

## Connect with like-minded people

Gaga feels a real kinship to the gay community. Early in her career, gay nightclubs in New York City and around the country took a chance on an unknown singer. She had a hard time getting radio airplay, so she was extremely grateful to the gay community for supporting her when no one else would. "The turning point for me was the gay community," Gaga told MTV. "I've got so many gay fans and they're so loyal to me and they really lifted me up. They'll always stand by me and I'll always stand by them. It's not an easy thing to create a fan base. . . . Being invited to play [the San Francisco Pride rally], that was a real turning point for me as an artist."

Her affection for her gay fans caused her to use her growing celebrity to advocate for equality issues. She has spoken at rallies in support of the repeal of the "Don't Ask, Don't Tell" (DADT) policy barring gays from openly serving in the military. She supports marriage equality. In collaboration with Cyndi Lauper, Gaga joined forces with MAC Cosmetics to launch a line of lipstick under their supplementary cosmetic line, Viva Glam. All net proceeds of the lipstick line were donated to the cosmetic company's campaign to prevent HIV and AIDS worldwide. "My love for my gay fans is just pure, authentic love for them as supporters of me from the beginning, and me feeling connected to their struggles as someone who is a part of their fight," she has said. She has advocated for these fans, and a loyal community of like-minded people has rallied around her as a result.

Gaga also has connected with young people who have been ostracized and bullied, whether they were gay or straight, because she endured repeated cruelty by peers during her teenage years. In lesson 2, we learned she was thrown into a trash can by bullies in her neighborhood. She was made fun of and called names by schoolmates. "I was called really horrible, profane names very loudly in front of huge crowds of people, and my schoolwork suffered at one point," she told Nicholas Kristof of *The New York Times*. "I didn't want to go to class. And I was a straight-A student, so there was a certain point in my high school years where I just couldn't even focus on class because I was so embarrassed all the time. I was so ashamed of who I was." Many of her fans connect with this feeling.

Gaga says she feels her audience is an army of outsiders. "It's funny because some friends of mine from New York, they all came out to see [last weekend's] show in New York. And they all said to me, 'Gaga, your fans are all of the misfits. They are all of the kids in school that everybody makes fun of,'" she explained to MTV. "All of the weird kids, the artistic kids, all the bad ones. And I love that, because that's who I was. We're all together and they get it. It's our own little world." Even Gaga understands that creating their own little world together unites fans. She connects so well with her fan community because she is one of them. She understands their struggles and communicates that understanding to them. She has made herself, in essence, a peer.

### Be authentic

One of the keys to building close-knit connections is for the leader of the community to show his or her real self, warts, flaws, and all. They need to be authentic, not always perfect. And they need to be accessible to fans. For example, Gaga's manager, Troy Carter, confirms that the singer is the only one who has the "keys" to her Twitter account. It is really *her* tweeting to fans, and she tweets often. She tweets directly to fans that ask her questions, shares photos from backstage and at her hotel, and gives updates on what is going on with her as she travels the world on her concert tours. One of the most viewed photos she ever tweeted was one in which she had no makeup on—a rare occurrence for a woman who is usually made up like a drag queen.

Gaga often posts personal messages to fans about how she is feeling on Littlemonsters.com, her own personal network for the One Percenters. She has shared with them the heartbreak of betrayal of lifelong friends and mentors who have taken advantage of her. She laments about her "massive struggles with [her] body image." She has shared personal details of time spent with her boyfriend, actor Taylor Kinney. She thanks fans for being there through good times and bad. She is open, raw, and real, and it is apparent by reading the comments and fan letters online that although most of them have never met her, they feel they know exactly who she is. It's these kinds of posts on Littlemonsters.com that elicit the most comments. Fans console the pop star, telling her that she doesn't need to lose weight and that she is beautiful just as she is. They tell her not to dwell on the betrayals and that they will always be there to support her.

While Gaga is fastidious about putting together an avant-garde ensemble, she occasionally lets her hair down and gets emotional in front of fans, which endears her to them even more. In 2011, HBO produced a two-hour documentary called *Lady Gaga Presents: The Monster Ball Tour at Madison Square Garden*, which featured concert footage as well as preconcert and backstage content. One of the preconcert scenes captured Gaga sitting at a mirror, taking off her existing makeup so new makeup could be applied. Feeling the pressure of performing at such a high-profile venue in her hometown of New York City seemed to be weighing on her. She mentioned to her makeup artists that she was in a bad mood on the way to the venue. She then gets emotional talking about how even though she is playing in one of the most iconic venues of her career, she sometimes doesn't feel worthy of her success. Through sobs, she says,

> I start to think about all of the people that have tried to stop me, and I get this, like, super-intense fury. Yeah, then I think about how I don't really give a shit if people don't understand what I do, as long as my fans understand. . . . I just sometimes feel like a loser still, you know? It's crazy, because it's like, we're at the Garden, but I still sometimes feel like a loser kid in high school. I've just got to pick my shit up, I've got to pick myself up, and I have to tell myself I'm a superstar every morn-

ing so that I can get through this day, and be for my
fans what they need for me to be.

"She's done a masterful job about creating an engaged community," says Erin Nelson, chief marketing officer for Austin,
Texas–based technology company Bazaarvoice. Bazaarvoice
brought Gaga's manager, Troy Carter, to Austin to speak to the
entire employee base to share insights about how the singer connects with her fans. Nelson says, "She's done a tremendous job,
I think, of understanding where her fans are, and then figuring
out how to make herself accessible and engaged, so she keeps
building them along the way. I think every Little Monster out
there, honestly, does feel like they've got a personal connection
to Lady Gaga." While it is easy for bigger-than-life rock stars to
seem out of reach and inaccessible, Gaga somehow balances being the Queen of Pop with being a real person that people can
actually interact with and feel they know personally.

### Create a collective experience

Another way to weave more connections into a community is
to create a collective experience, something that members can
encounter together. This creates bonds as members relive the
experience over the years. One way Gaga does this is with her
concert tours. The concert tours for each album have all been
named "balls," as in the Fame Ball Tour, the Monster Ball
Tour, and the Born This Way Ball Tour. She uses the word "ball"

to connote a fun, joyous, dance-filled event. I attended two concerts during the Monster Ball Tour and I can attest to it being like a loud, giant costume party. The majority of the audience was dressed in iconic Gaga outfits from her videos and TV appearances. Gaga told Larry King,

> The Monster Ball is in essence an exorcism for my fans and for myself where we sort of put everything out on the table and reject it. There is so much in the show about insecurity and struggle. And so many of my fans are really, really, really troubled. And I was really troubled. And I still am fairly troubled. So I guess you can say I relate to my fans in that way. And I choose not to hide from it. I'm not interested, Larry, in being a perfect placid pop singer that looks great in bikinis and is on the cover of every magazine. I'm more interested in helping my fans to love who they are and helping them to reject prejudice and reject those things that they're taught from society to not like themselves.

During the Monster Ball concerts, she speaks to the audience, telling them the type of experience she aims to create:

> The Monster Ball will set you free! And the best thing about the Monster Ball is that I created it so my fans have a place to go. A place where all the freaks are outside and I lock the fucking doors. It don't matter who you are, where you come from, or how much

money you got in your pocket because tonight and every other after night you could be whoever it is that you want to be.

While her concerts are giant lovefests in the name of all things Gaga, she sprinkles messages of self-awareness and hope between the songs. Her message to the audience is to inspire them to love themselves more and more fearlessly despite conditions that lead to lack of self-worth. "What I do is, in essence, create an atmosphere for my fans where they don't leave loving me, they leave loving themselves," she told MTV.

In-person events are a great way to create a collective experience. But online experiences can really scale. As we discussed earlier, Gaga gathers her superfans together and interacts with them in a private online community, Littlemonsters.com. The first thing you see when you sign in to to Littlemonsters.com is a picture of Gaga with the message "Welcome Home, Little Monsters!" Fans are encouraged to "share [their] passion and creativity in a community full of art, acceptance, monsters and Gaga."

To be able to have a collective experience in the community means that fans should be able to talk to one another. Because Gaga's fans span all corners of the globe, the chat feature on Littlemonsters.com translates fifty-seven languages in real time so fans can understand one another.

## Celebrate milestones

Celebrating important milestones and achievements together reinforces a feeling of community among its members. As the leader of the fan community, Gaga shares her achievements but presents them as milestones that the community has achieved together. For example, on October 24, 2011, when the collective views of all the videos on Gaga's YouTube channel reached one billion, she celebrated with fans, tweeting, "We reached 1 Billion views on youtube little monsters! If we stick together we can do anything. I dub u kings and queens of youtube! Unite!"

When the album *Born This Way* was nominated for three Grammy Awards in 2011, Gaga thanked the fans. She tweeted, "I'm humbled + honored to have a Trinity of nominations from the Grammy's, including Album of the Year for Born This Way. I love u so much." In a follow-up tweet, she said, "#PawsUp for our album's being nominated three years in a row. I could never do it without you. Together, we were #BornToBeBrave." Notice the use of the word "our" as in "our album." She wanted the fans to know that since she wrote the album for them, it was essentially their album, too. And now their album was being recognized for being one of the best that year. This was retweeted 7,881 times by fans.

Another milestone that Gaga celebrated with fans was about the number of members of Littlemonsters.com. On August 25, 2012, she tweeted that Littlemonsters.com had just reached five hundred thousand members. Fans retweeted this achievement 4,796 times. The key to commemorating milestones with customers is to celebrate achievements that are common to the community. Fans reacted to aforementioned tweets by Gaga by congratulating not only the singer but themselves as well. They know that they contributed to the achievement and share in the joy that Gaga feels.

### Encourage collaboration

A terrific way to cement bonds within a community is to get members to work together on projects. This allows customers to work toward something collectively, and in the end everyone can celebrate when they accomplish their goal.

In May 2011, Gaga was working on a short film to be used as an ad for Google's web browser Chrome. She doesn't appear in many ads but she was doing a favor for a friend who was a Google executive. Plus, the video would help promote her new single, "The Edge of Glory." The premise of the film was to "celebrate Lady Gaga's special and unmediated relationship with her fans, the Little Monsters." The single launched on May 9, 2012, and fans immediately began uploading YouTube videos of themselves dancing to it, singing it, and playing it on all kinds of instruments. Gaga then posted a message on her Web site, asking for more videos to be used in the film. Fans responded within minutes and uploaded hundreds more videos. Back in the editing room, in real time as fan videos streamed in, editors were putting them into the film. Gaga's team collected more than eighty thousand YouTube clips from fans. The whole project took less than ten days to produce, just in time to air during Gaga's performance on the season finale of *Saturday Night Live.*

As of this writing, Gaga is conducting a number of contests on Littlemonsters.com to encourage fans to work on projects. One project involves designing a new outfit for Gaga to wear. Fans must enter their submission on their Littlemonsters.com profile, and Gaga and her team, as well as all Little Monsters in the community, will judge submissions. Another contest invites fans to design emoticons that will be used in the chat function of Littlemonsters.com. All of these submissions appear on the front "wall" or feed of the site daily for other Monsters to "like" and comment on.

Gaga is not the only one encouraging fans to collaborate. Fans themselves are coming up with projects and encouraging other fans to participate. In March 2010, Ryan James Yezak, a fan and young filmmaker from Los Angeles, asked fans to help make a video for Gaga's twenty-fourth birthday. Yezak spliced together video clips of birthday messages from 128 Little Monsters from around the world into an almost ten-minute-long video. Many of the messages included comments about Gaga and how her music had changed their lives. Gaga got wind of the video and tweeted a link to the video and said "I've never cried so hard in 24 years, from pure joy and unconditional love. Tears still streaming."

Similarly, three seventeen-year-old girls from Boston created the "Dear Mother Monster Project." They asked fans to address letters to Gaga and tell them about the impact she has had on their lives. Fans posted letters online to a Tumblr site that the girls had set up. They were overwhelmed and inspired by the responses that were filled with personal stories of hope and love. (Many of the fan quotes in this book are from that site.) Fans also sent the girls video messages explaining what Mother Monster means to them. In heartfelt messages, and sometimes while crying, Little Monsters poured their hearts out to help Gaga understand how her existence had changed their lives. The girls posted the eight-minute video to YouTube, titled "Dear Mother Monster: A thank you from all your fans," and then to Littlemonsters.com. Gaga watched the video, was apparently speechless, and initially left a two-word comment on the video post: "Can't breathe." Later she posted a comment telling the girls she couldn't wait to meet them at the Boston Born This Way Ball Tour stop and invited them backstage. One commenter on the "Dear Mother Monster Project" video summed it up nicely: "Your little monsters love you so much. And for us it's not really about your cute tweets or your fashion choices. It's more about the music, and the community, and the things that you teach us."

Gaga could teach a class on community management, and other more traditional businesses out there are doing a good job of it, too. When we think about building community Gaga-style, two companies immediately come to mind as stellar examples of embracing customers within existing fan communities: Fiskars and MINI. These two companies, while different in product and customer base, both listen to what customers are saying to one another so that they can identify how customers talk about their products and connect to the passion customers have for sharing meaningful experiences with one another.

## Business example: Fiskars

Let's start with Fiskars and their community of One Percenters called the Fiskateers. Fiskars is a Finnish housewares company started in 1649, making it one of the oldest businesses in the Western world. Fiskars sells knives, utensils, cookware, and cutlery but is best known for its orange-handled scissors. The craft division of Fiskars had very low brand loyalty since Chinese companies copied their products—crafting tools and consumables—as soon as they hit the market. Fiskars' own brand research revealed that they were the "milk and saltine crackers" of their industry, with little emotional connection to customers.

Fiskars wanted to create a relationship between the company and its customers that went beyond tools. The company hired branding agency Brains on Fire to help them understand their customers better and connect with them. Brains on Fire set up 150 interviews with members of Yahoo! crafting groups and joined conversations about crafting on message boards and other online communities. The agency's research found a social and robust crafting community, especially among scrapbookers. The agency recommended creating a branded community program to embrace the existing passionate scrapbookers in the United States. The program is called the Fiskateers, and the company set out to find scrapbookers who could serve as ambassadors of the brand to the community.

Fiskars (with the help of Brains on Fire) did a "four-city casting call for the loudest, proudest paper crafters across the country." During a road trip that included eleven cities, over one hundred people stepped forward to tell their stories and show their creative crafting personalities. What the road trip showed Fiskars was that the crafting community wanted better ways to connect to one another and, according to Fiskars, longed for "a new type of crafting community . . . that was uplifting and encouraging, where members could feel safe to share about themselves, shine a spotlight on their handiwork, and talk openly about the tools they use to create it."

They then chose the most passionate ambassadors that they found in the scrapbooking community and put the spotlight on four women who eventually became known as the "Fab Four" lead Fiskateers. These women were able to recruit other scrapbookers into the community and, according to Fiskars, over two hundred people joined the Fiskateer movement in its first twenty-four hours. And the people who joined were not saying, "Oh my gosh! These scissors are fantastic. I want to join a club for scrapbooking scissors." They were joining because of their love of scrapbooking and their desire to connect with other passionate scrapbookers. They oriented the community program around this passion, not selling more products. Sales of products are a by-product of creating a loyal customer community that wants to spread the word to other people.

In crafting the Fiskateers program, the company, like Gaga, understood the use of offline and online collective experiences. The company created a membership-only online community where crafters could set up profiles, converse with one another, and upload photos of their designs. Fiskars also orchestrates offline events that get people together who may have only met online. For example, during the first year of the program, they brought the top fifty most active and passionate crafters to San Antonio, Texas, to learn how to expand their role as a "crafting ambassador." They were taught certified demonstrator classes and encouraged to certify at least twenty people in their own communities, creating a one-thousand-person army of Certified Fiskars Demonstrators (CFDs). Stores like Walmart and Michaels had been asking Fiskars to teach classes at their stores, and now Fiskars had a list of teachers. Walmart pays the CFD to teach the class, Fiskars gets exposure, Fiskateers get to teach the hobby they love to others, and sales at the store increase. It's a win-win-win situation. And to keep the momentum going Fiskars created regional offline events called Fiskafriendzy where crafters can get together with people they live close to. They may meet these other Fiskateers online, but then they're able to connect offline. And that helps really cement the bonds of this core group. As comments in a YouTube video from a scrapbooker entitled "Why I Love Being a Fiskateer" show, the community has a very strong bond: "There's a genuine love, care and concern toward other Fiskateers. It's a wonderful place to be. I have to check in every day . . . It's not about just friendships anymore. It's more about a camaraderie and a family feeling now. But the number one thing [I love about Fiskateers] is I believe I am free to be me. It's a very welcoming community. I really do love it."

Fiskars has seen a tremendous return on investing in their customer community. There are now more than seven thousand members of the Fiskateers community, and each one is a brand ambassador who spreads the message to other crafters. Branded mentions of Fiskars products online are up more than 600 percent since the start of the program. Sales have doubled in cities with Fiskateers compared to non-Fiskateer cities. And an unexpected bonus: On average, the company receives thirteen new ideas for products per month, for free.

Fiskars' Fiskateers program is a terrific example of how to build a sense of community within a customer base. The company understood that it's important to first be a member of the customer community instead of building an online community and hoping people will join. That's why they visited cities to talk with crafters in person and joined in conversations online in crafting forums before putting together the Fiskateers program. It's important to understand customers' passions and how they relate to one another. Then you can begin to devise a community program that isn't just focused on you and your products. It's focused on people. People are more likely to be loyal to people than inanimate brands. And if you can make that personal, emotional connection happen between people, that's something a product alone can't do.

## Business example: MINI

What's a graceful way to move from scissor enthusiasts to car enthusiasts? Well, there is no graceful way except to say that when it comes to the power of communities to help elevate brands, nothing stops crafters and nothing stops drivers. I know this firsthand. Not because I own Fiskars scissors, but because I have a MINI Cooper, and I love it. I love MINI's sense of style, I love their marketing, and I love the car. I bought my first MINI in 2004 because I loved the design and because it was the only car that would fit in my tiny one-car garage in Chicago. In January 2012, the old MINI was starting to decline, and I decided to buy a new car. My short list included the Toyota Prius, the Lexus IS, and, for good measure, another MINI.

It just so happens that there's a MINI Meetup group in Austin, where I live. Meetups are interest groups that use the Web site Meetup.com to connect. There are seven hundred people in the Austin MINI Meetup group, and I just happened to meet a woman who runs it at a party about the time I was deciding to buy a car. Now, she doesn't work for MINI. She's just a volunteer who started the group. Every month, Meetup members participate in three or four activities, like driving the back roads from Austin to Lockhart, the BBQ capital of Texas, or participating in local parades. That sold me on the MINI because I thought, "You know what? Not only am I buying a MINI, but I'm buying possible relationships and experiences with all these people who love the same thing I do, which is this cute little fun-to-drive car."

As we learned in the Fiskars example, the key to building community is first to listen to customers and understand their passions. Tom O'Brien of online research company MotiveQuest has tapped into MINI owners' conversations on the Web to build a profile—a profile that actually looks a lot like me. He found that while customers talked about things like car performance and customization, they actually talked more about social topics, such as other enthusiasts, clubs, and events and gatherings. O'Brien describes MINI customers as a tribal community. He says, "In the MINI community it's all about belonging or showing off . . . you create loyalty in the MINI community by giving them more opportunities to interact with each other and find and participate with the MINI tribe." And that is what MINI is doing.

MINI has regional clubs, each started independently, which count MINI car enthusiasts as their members. All it takes to join is the love of driving and the love of the MINI. These clubs began independently and continue to be independent of MINI, but the company has found innovative ways to tap into these communities, to create common links between them, and to act as a sort of common meeting place for them on its Web site. Under the heading "WHY MINI" on MINIUSA.com is a link to over sixty owner clubs in the United States, a map by region, and a link to contact the company about clubs it might not know about. Each club's page is directly linked and the setup makes the clubs feel endorsed by MINI.

For the past four years, the company has held an annual event called MINI Takes the States, an eleven-day cross-country trek where MINI owners meet up for food and music. It's a kind of tribal "let's get together and show off our MINIs" event, says O'Brien. In 2012, approximately six thousand people signed up to participate in at least one of the eighty-eight events on the trek, while up to three hundred cars could be spotted on one stretch of road. From New York to Los Angeles, the route wound through sixteen states with stops in thirteen cities and covered at least 3,877 miles. Some eighty-nine people drove the whole thing.

MINI believes that the secret to selling more cars is to engage the existing MINI community rather than to target people who currently don't own MINIs. They believe that if they can get current owners more excited about the brand, they will sell more cars to them. And the owners will sell more cars to new customers through word of mouth. That's why so much of their marketing involves helping MINI enthusiasts find one another in independent clubs and at MINI-sponsored events. And the strategy seems to be working. Its June 2012 sales were up 14.7 percent compared to the same month the previous year, and it's running 7.5 percent higher for the year, compared with 2011. The British icon now owned by BMW is on pace to sell more than sixty thousand units in 2012. It also won the Polk Automobile Loyalty Award in 2009 and 2010 for highest repeat purchase rates among current customers in the compact-car category. I'm one of those loyal customers. I ended up getting a brand-new MINI model, the sporty Coupe. It looks like the original MINI Cooper's sexy, seductive cousin.

||||||||||||||||||

Building a community of fans or customers doesn't happen overnight. As Gaga and anyone else who is a community manager knows, it takes hard work every day to connect with those who are of like minds and to nurture relationships with them. It takes an egoless spirit to show the community that your company is not just concerned with financial gain but also with what's in the best interest of the community. Once you sense that customers want to be part of something more than a transactional relationship, you can begin the process of helping them self-identify. The next step, as we're about to see in Lesson 4, is to give the community an identity. To give them a name.

# Give Fans a Name

"We identify with each other, I see myself in my fans and my fans see themselves in me. I call them little monsters because they are my inspiration."

**— Lady Gaga**

**W**hat's in a name? Creating a name for your One Percenters assigns them an identity, and with that identity comes a set of recognizable behavioral or personal characteristics that everyone with that name shares. As a result people will self-identify as part of the group, or recognize that they are outside the group. In essence, a name gives your fans something to join, to be part of. The simple act of referring to themselves by the name gives customers a sense of belonging.

Gaga calls her fans the Little Monsters, but she didn't set out to think up a name for them. The name came organically. Gaga explained to Larry King,

> I wrote the album *The Fame Monster*, which is the second album. And when I had finished, I realized that I had written each song about a particular fear that I had come across on my journey promoting *The Fame* [the first album]. And then when I went on tour, my fans were so—they were salivating at the mouth and they couldn't—they were rabid. They couldn't wait for me to sing my new songs, and they just behaved like monsters on—in the audience. So a couple of nights I just said, "You little monsters," . . . I had used the lyric

on the album as well, little monsters. So I just started calling them my little monsters.

And so a name for her most loyal fans was born.

Gaga has used high-profile events to show her dedication to these Little Monsters. Gaga performed at the 52nd Annual Grammy Awards on January 31, 2010. She was to sing for the first time with Elton John and had commissioned a special piano for the performance. The dual-sided Baldwin piano allowed Gaga and John to sit on each side while playing and singing to each other. The most striking feature of the piano were eerie black claw-hand arms jutting upward from the top (see Fig. 4.1).

**Fig. 4.1** Elton John, left, and Lady Gaga perform at the 52nd Annual Grammy Awards using a Terence Koh–designed piano. *(Matt Sayles / AP Photo)*

While at the show, Gaga tweeted a photo (similar to the one below) of her and John performing, saying "piano designed [by] the famous and dear friend TERENCE KOH, inspired by and in honor of my little monsters, and their sweet little hands."

Terence Koh, a Canadian artist who was born in China, explained the idea behind the strange-looking piano: "The hands were based on sculptures of hands I had done in a previous exhibition. Lady Gaga and I then thought it would be great for the hands to be claw-like, in dedication to her fans making a claw-shaped 'monster hand.' It was an homage to when you go to her concerts and you see a wave of those hands, which Lady Gaga calls her 'little monsters.' It was about a sea of love and affection."

At the Grammys that night, Gaga went on to win Best Electronic/Dance Album for *The Fame* and Best Dance Recording for the song "Poker Face." Hours after the show, she shared the night's recognition with the fans, tweeting "We won big tonight little monsters, I am so proud to make music 4 you. I hope I continue to inspire u the way u inspire me. You're everything." The next day she tweeted a photo of a new tattoo on the inside of her left forearm. The tattoo was the words "Little Monsters" in a script font. Her tweet explained, "look what i did last night. little monsters forever, on the arm that holds my mic. xx." Little Monsters forever. It said a lot. Gaga was telling fans that they were part of her by etching the Little Monsters' name in perpetuity on her body. And that they would be part of her every day for the rest of her life. The fans saw the commitment that she had just made to them. Many of them decided to make the same commitment to her. They began tweeting photos of Little Monsters tattoos that they themselves had gotten. They had, in effect, branded themselves part of Gaga's army of monsters. Sometimes it really is all in a name.

It wasn't just the fans that got a name. As the Little Monsters' affection for Gaga grew, many began to see her as a mother figure and started referring to her as "Mother Monster." *Forbes* writer Judy Martin likened Gaga to "the Kali-esque figure in Hinduism, so black that she can absorb any negativity and eat it up, all while wielding a sword to protect her young children." Gaga metaphorically protects the bullied misfits who were teased, as she was in school. She uses her concerts as a safe haven for those who feel they don't belong, or are called freaks or weirdos by others. She embraces another, more powerful name for them when she calls them Little Monsters. She openly shows her love and affection for fans and wants to protect them.

There are conflicting stories about how Gaga began to be called Mother Monster by her fans. Lore has it that a fan who met her backstage in Chicago used the term. Then Gaga adopted the moniker and stylized it as Mother Mons†er, which now is her screen name on Littlemonsters.com.

Naming customers gives them an identity that is connected to you. It gives them a way to refer to one another as being in a sort of club or inner circle. Those who are attracted to your brand see that there is something to join because the customer community has a moniker. Lady Gaga doesn't have the monopoly on successful naming, but she wins for style and uniqueness. While she has a lot to teach us about the power of the name—her own as Mother Monster and her fans' as Little Monsters—other companies have been successful in the act of naming their customers or fans. The history of Maker's Mark Ambassadors and the recent embracing and expansion of the Aruba Airheads name and community are two great examples of the power of the name.

## Business example: Maker's Mark Ambassadors

When the Samuels family of Loretto, Kentucky, started selling their small-batch bourbon in 1954, they were selling it to their friends and family. In a classic word-of-mouth story, their friends started telling friends about Maker's Mark bourbon, and over the years they built a cult fan base. They began to distribute their product across the country and millions began enjoying the premium bourbon. Bill Samuels Jr., the son of the founder, tells what happened next in an interview he did with my podcast partner, Ben McConnell, and me in 2006:

> Maker's [had] started to develop in every metropolitan center in the country, at the same pace, essentially. Even in Idaho there is a group of young professionals that picked up on it. It was all word of mouth, because there was no way for us to reach them, find them, talk to them. They weren't talking to us, but they were talking to friends of friends of the brand. I don't know how many there was in there and we couldn't ever track it. It

started to bother me that we were not going to be able to have the same personal relationship with our friends, with our recommenders, as we had had in Kentucky.

In 2000, a brainstorm hit. Bill Samuels told us, "I got an idea that . . . will allow us to connect with our fanatical customers, outside of the Kentucky cocktail party circuit." This idea was to bestow ambassadorship onto their One Percenters and find a way to connect with them. The Maker's Mark Ambassador program was born. The Ambassadors were in effect those fanatical Maker's Mark customers who volunteered to tell others about the product and also encourage bars that didn't carry the brand at the time to do so.

Marker's Mark has built what I believe to be one of the best loyalty programs out there today, and they've been doing this for twelve years! When you sign up to be an Ambassador, the first thing you get is a welcome kit that contains custom business cards with your name on them, identifying you as an official Ambassador. The welcome kit also contains a "Barrel Dedication Certificate" explaining that your name has just been engraved on a barrel of bourbon that will age for six years in the historic distillery in Loretto, Kentucky. Along with the barrel number, the certificate proclaims that your name is on the barrel "in recognition of loyalty, outstanding dedication, in-depth knowledge and service as an honorable Maker's Mark Ambassador" (see Fig 4.2). When the barrel is done being aged, Ambassadors receive an invitation to come to the Loretto dis-

**Fig. 4.2** Maker's Mark welcome kit for a new Maker's Mark Ambassador *(courtesy of Jason Reeves)*

tillery along with their barrelmates to sample a batch made from their special cask.

Those wishing to sign up as an Ambassador can go the Maker's Mark Web site and click on "Embassy." They call it the Embassy, because if you are an Ambassador, where else would you hang out? New Ambassadors can download more business cards and even order a copy of their barrel plate. Longtime Ambassadors know to update their mailing information in the Embassy because Maker's Mark is known for the holiday gifts they send Ambassadors. Some of the more memorable gifts over the years have included an ice-ball mold for making giant spherical ice cubes for drinking chilled bourbon, and a knitted green, red, and white holiday sweater emblazoned with reindeer that fits perfectly on one's Maker's Mark bottle. The Samuels family apparently like to wear festive sweaters during the holidays, so they thought their Ambassadors' bottles might like one, too.

Maker's Mark management doesn't disclose how many Ambassadors are in the program because they want to keep the feeling that this is still just a small group of friends. But my guess is that it is in the hundreds of thousands. Still, that is a small part of the millions of Maker's Mark drinkers in the world. When asked about spending money and resources on creating a program for just 1 percent of their customer base, Bill Samuels Jr. told us, "We never worry about the fact that, 'Oh my God, this is inefficient, because we are only talking to fifty or sixty, or a thousand or ten thousand, instead of a million,' which you do when you try to slap everybody on the ass with an advertising message. We know that our next customers are going to come from [our Ambassadors'] efforts, not from our efforts."

By giving One Percenters a name, people can self-identify as superfans by adopting the name for themselves. When I make my keynote presentations, I ask, "Who here is a Lady Gaga fan?" and some hands go up. When I ask, "Which one of you would consider yourself a Little Monster?" a smaller set of people raise their hands. Lady Gaga fans understand what being a Little Monster entails. They can draw that line between casual fan and fanatic and put themselves in one of those categories. Just like with Maker's Mark Ambassadors, only the people who really love the brand are going to raise their hands and want to participate and be engaged.

## Business example: Aruba Networks

Another interesting example of the power of naming customers is the "Airheads" community, launched in December 2011 by Aruba Networks, a leading provider of next-generation network access solutions for the mobile enterprise. The company's Mobile Virtual Enterprise (MOVE) architecture unifies wired and wireless network infrastructures into one seamless access solution for corporate headquarters, mobile business professionals, remote workers, and guests. Say what? In non-geek-speak, Aruba helps companies deal with employees who want to use all manner of mobile devices such as iPhones and iPads to access their corporate e-mail, databases, and other networks.

Aruba Networks came up with the idea to officially recognize and grow an existing community of the most avid network engineers. These engineers are part of IT teams around the world that are dealing with the trend of "bring your own device" to work. This trend is making corporate networks a bear to manage. Companies need IT staff trained in the latest tools for wireless LAN, security, and mobile device management to deal with it. Aruba has tools and solutions for just this challenge and wanted to connect better with the community of engineers who use their products. Aruba ironically named these extremely intelligent, technically trained folks "Airheads" because their work deals with wireless networking, or networking through the air. Dayle Hall, Aruba Networks senior director of corporate marketing and corporate communications, says that all technical experts in mobility and wireless, not just Aruba customers, are welcome in the community. This is why the Airheads name and logo takes a lead role on the program's Web site and at events while Aruba's corporate branding is deemphasized.

Like Maker's Mark Ambassadors, Aruba Airheads receive special perks for joining the community. There are over ten thousand Airheads worldwide, and they have access to a wide variety of professional development opportunities, including:

- Airheads Social, a private social-media platform that acts as the central hub for all Airheads community activities

- Aruba Certification and Training Program, which prepares engineers to solve a host of complex challenges that extend well beyond the wired infrastructure

- Airheads events that allow members to collaborate in real time with other members at the annual Airheads conferences, regional user-group events, and virtual events

- Aruba Airheads MVP Program, which recognizes members who have helped cultivate the Airheads community through their expertise, participation, and contributions; the more engaged members are with all aspects of the community, the more rewards and recognition they receive

The Airhead events are where members get together to share information, connect, and recognize other members of their community. Members attending receive the benefits of the program firsthand and feel like they are part of a club of like-minded, tech-savvy people. The events are both face-to-face and virtual and allow network engineers to collaborate on best practices, real-world deployment examples, and lessons learned. These include annual regional conferences with hundreds of attendees, quarterly half-day events in cities around the globe, and exclusive online webinars delivered by Airheads MVPs and experts. Zach Jennings, an Airheads MVP and senior network server manager for West Chester University of Pennsylvania, says, "Within the Airheads community, I can share my experience to help others. . . . Another key benefit is learning. Reading posts from other users exposes me to a world of possibilities."

||||||||||||||||||||

Whether it's Little Monsters, Ambassadors, or Airheads, the power in a name is most obvious to the people that self-identify using it. A name provides them access to one another, to an elite community of like-minded people. It gives them perks that those outside the community don't get to enjoy, and it helps remind them that the social aspect of any endeavor can be a powerful thing. We all want to be members of the club. It's that feeling of belonging that gives us energy and enthusiasm for what we do.

Having a name also strengthens the bond between customers because they immediately recognize one another's membership in an exclusive club. Another way to strengthen these bonds is by using shared symbols, often connected to the name of the community or the activities that community participates in. Only the people who are part of the named One Percenters understand these symbols, discussed next in Lesson 5.

# Embrace Shared Symbols

"I . . . try to create things that are quite easy for my
fans to replicate . . . and that bonds us in a way.
It's quite nice to have this connection to them
outside of everything else."

— **Lady Gaga**

Studies of cultures and societies often show an emergence of shared symbols. We can all visualize many symbols we share with others as members of a given group, city, or country. These shared symbols are tangible vehicles through which some meaning is expressed. The symbols could be gestural, pictorial, object-oriented, linguistic, or some combination of these. Through the repeated process of rituals, symbols are given significance in the group. Shared symbols also have the ability to be exclusionary. Those who can recognize and understand the meaning of these symbols feel part of the group, like they belong, while outsiders will not understand the meaning and turn away, sometimes mocking the symbols.

Businesses understand the power of branding and creating memorable brand images for their products. While brands can be one type of symbol, they don't go nearly far enough in building connections between people. Brands are simply a product identifier. Lady Gaga is a master of these other types of symbols—symbols that are not directly related to a product but are more about a shared experience.

There are a number of shared symbols in the Little Monsters society. Most have been created by Gaga and appropriated by fans. Gaga has a very keen sense of art and iconic visuals. She uses these visuals in her clothing, her choreography, her concert stages, and her video sets, all of which she has a direct hand in designing. To help ideate and create these iconic visuals, the singer formed the Haus of Gaga, her personal creative team responsible for much of her distinctive and individual style. The Haus is based on Andy Warhol's Factory and emulates the creative atmosphere it was known for. This team creates most of the clothing, props, stage sets, and makeup for Gaga's live performances and other visual representations of her work, as well as individual pieces that artistically represent the style and themes emphasized by Gaga. Some of the Haus's more famous pieces include the "disco stick" (a long chrome pole with a crushed acrylic dome that emits light), the "iPod LCD glasses" (a pair of glasses with two iPod Classic screens instead of lenses), and the "meat dress" worn at the 2010 MTV Video Music Awards. Gaga and her creative team work tirelessly, thinking about the meanings and symbolic nature of what she creates and embraces. Let's walk through some of the most recognizable symbols in the Little Monster community.

## Monster Paw

The most universally known symbol of the Little Monsters is the monster paw. The monster paw is a hand sign formed by spacing the fingers apart and contorting them, as if imitating the claw of an animal, or—more fittingly—a monster. The origins of the monster paw stem from the award-winning chore-ography in Gaga's iconic video for the song "Bad Romance." In various segments of the video, Gaga and a throng of dancers are seen dancing with clawed hands. The video became a huge hit, especially on YouTube, and Gaga fans everywhere began learning the distinctive dance moves.

Soon Gaga discovered the clawed hand had become more than just a dance move. During the Monster Ball Tour, Gaga would often relate this story: She was being driven through Boston for one of her concert stops there. Her car pulled up to a stoplight and in the car beside her, with the windows down, is a fan dancing and singing to a Gaga song blasting on the car stereo. She's about to roll down the window to get the person's attention, but before she can do that, another car pulls up on the other side of the car that is blasting the music. The window rolls down and out of the second car shoots a clawed hand. Gaga said, "It was a very exciting moment because my fan was so excited that they had seen another Little Monster and that they felt compelled to let them know that 'I, too, am a Lady Gaga fan.' So on that day, we declared that [the claw hand] is the symbol of a Lady Gaga fan." During the Monster Ball Tour, Gaga would call for the Little Monsters to put their "paws up," referring to the clawed hand (see Fig. 5.1). Now, "Paws up!" has become a phrase used by Gaga and Little Monsters everywhere to mean "high five" or "good job." Gaga even put a reference to the monster paw in the lyrics to her song "Born This Way," opening the song with:

**Fig. 5.1** Little Monsters with paws up at the Manila, Philippines, stop on the Born This Way Ball Tour, May 21, 2012 *(Jay Directo / AFP / Getty Images)*

*It doesn't matter if you love him, or capital H-I-M*
*Just put your paws up*
*'Cause you were born this way, baby.*

## The Unicorn

Gaga has a thing for unicorns. She told the *Big Top 40 Show* in England that she's "obsessed with the idea of a creature that was born with something magical that sort of made them the misfit in the world of the stallion." Elaborating further on her fascination, she commented: "They are in essence a mythical creature, so what I'm trying to say is the unicorn was born magical and it's not the unicorn's fault and it doesn't make it any more or less special or any less unique but it can't help that it was born with that magic." The unicorn symbol was introduced to the Little Monsters through the album *Born This Way*. When the album came out, Gaga got a tattoo of a unicorn head with a banner that said "Born This Way" wrapped around its large pointed horn. There is also a song on the album called "Highway Unicorn," and Gaga tweeted to a fan that "Highway Unicorn is about me. Flying down the road, with nothing but a dream," and for the performance of the song on her Born This Way Ball Tour, Gaga entered the stage on a giant mechanical unicorn. Fans have adopted the symbol and created fan art incorporating unicorns. Gaga tweeted an amazing piece of fan art that merged Gaga's head and torso with a unicorn body. Fans bring stuffed unicorns to Gaga's concerts and throw them onstage or present them as gifts to her backstage.

## How Gaga Does It: Turning Experience into Symbols

Perhaps what makes Lady Gaga so adept at creating symbols that have longevity with her fans is her ability to find meaning in situations, experiences, and interactions and to turn that meaning into visuals. She creates iconic imagery by under-standing the power of images already out there and manipulat-ing them to fit her ethos. In her "Born This Way" video, she cast Rick Genest, a twenty-five-year-old homeless man from Montreal, Canada. He has his body tattooed from the waist up to the very top of his head to look like a decomposing corpse with the skeleton exposed. Lady Gaga's stylist, Nicola Formichetti, had discovered a photo of Genest while browsing through Google images and located him on Facebook. Then—and this is where she is a master of creating symbols—she used him in the video. For the video, Gaga's face is made up to look like a decomposing corpse with exposed skull, just like Genest's. She donned a giant pink ponytailed wig that stuck out of the top of her head above the makeup. Dressed in a tux, Gaga dances around an emotionless Genest in several scenes in the video. She was able to take the meaning of this twenty-five-year-old homeless man (and homelessness is a cause she supports and gives to because of the high percentage of LGBT teenagers who are homeless) and make it part of herself. Little Monsters know this imagery of the "ponytailed Gaga skull" from the video well. It is striking and memorable, and ultimately iconic. Gaga's team has used this image as the basis for the Monster Pit Key I'll discuss in the next chapter, and it has shown up on Gaga's perfume packaging as well. And of course, it can be seen on the bodies of many Little Monsters, as fans have internalized these symbols and actually gotten tattoos of them (see Fig. 5.2).

Gaga has become so good at embodying symbols that just about everything she puts on becomes one. But what makes them iconic is that each one has meaning for her. She doesn't create a symbol for the sake of creating symbols. She embraces

**Fig. 5.2** A fan's tattoo of the ponytailed Gaga skull symbol *(courtesy of Joel Diaz)*

something because of how meaningful it is to her. The examples outlined here, and many others too numerous to mention, come from her desire to make a statement about something important to her, and her fans immediately connect to it and embrace it.

There are also businesses and nonprofits out there doing a good job of creating symbols or embracing symbols already important to fans. The Steelers' Terrible Towel and Livestrong bracelets are two great examples of the power of symbols to change the game by bringing customers or fans together.

## Business example:
## Pittsburgh Steelers' Terrible Towel

Sports teams and symbolism go together like hot dogs and beer. You've got team logos, uniforms, mascots, and even hand signals. ("Hook 'em horns!") The best-known sports symbol, as deemed by ESPN, is the Terrible Towel, a gold rally towel used by the National Football League's Pittsburgh Steelers (see Fig. 5.3). Disclosure here: I was born just north of Pittsburgh and am a die-hard Steelers fan, so I can tell you firsthand what this symbol means to Steeler Nation. The towel was the brainchild of legendary radio announcer Myron Cope. Cope was a color commentator for the Steelers' radio broadcasts for thirty-five years. He was known for his distinctive, nasally voice and identifiable Pittsburgh accent, idiosyncratic speech pattern, and a level of excitement rarely exhibited in the broadcast booth. Prior to the Steelers' first playoff game of the 1975 season, Cope's bosses at the team's flagship radio station, WTAE, asked him to help invent a "gimmick" to attract more sponsors to his radio show. Cope was not interested, saying, "I am not a gimmick guy, never *have* been a gimmick guy." After his boss suggested that a successful gimmick would be good leverage for a raise in Cope's upcoming contract renewal, Cope replied, "I'm a gimmick guy."

Brainstorming with his boss, Cope said the gimmick should be something "lightweight and portable and already owned by just about every fan." His boss suggested towels. Cope thought

**Fig. 5.3** Pittsburgh Steelers Terrible Towel *(photo supplied by author)*

it was a great idea and said, "We'll call it the Terrible Towel and it will wreak its powers terribly on the opposition." Only some-one like the unique Myron Cope could imbue a towel with powers. In the weeks leading up to the game, Cope advertised the idea of the towel to fans on the radio and evening television news. "The Terrible Towel is poised to strike," Cope said over and over to his audiences. "Bring a yellow, gold or black towel to the playoff game, and if you don't have one, buy one, if you don't want to buy one, dye one."

The Terrible Towel made its first appearance on December 27, 1975, in a playoff game against the Baltimore Colts. In the broadcast booth, Cope had reason to be nervous. The local *Pittsburgh Post-Gazette* had mocked his towel idea. He saw less than a dozen towels while players were going through pregame warm-ups, even though two towels had been placed in each player's locker. "All of a sudden, a couple of fellows were trying, were sticking these yellow rags, these things in our hands and asking us to run on the field for introduction spinning them around," former Steelers safety Mike Wagner said. "We looked at the fellows and said, 'I don't think so. We're trying to play football here.'"

But Cope was vindicated. He recalls the event in his autobiography, *Double Yoi!* "Nearing kickoff, the Steelers gathered in their tunnel for introductions, whereupon the crowd exploded— and suddenly, by my estimation, 30,000 Terrible Towels twirled from the fists of fans around the stadium!" The Steelers went on to defeat the Colts 28–10. In the following weeks, the team defeated the Oakland Raiders and Dallas Cowboys to capture the franchise's second consecutive Super Bowl victory. And so the legend of the Terrible Towel was written. Every Pittsburgh Steelers fan has at least one. I have six. And fans often take them along on their journeys throughout the world. The Terrible Towel has been on *Saturday Night Live*, been waved at Vatican City, the Great Wall of China, and has traveled with soldiers in Iraq and Afghanistan. There was even a towel on the International Space Station, brought there by a Pittsburgh-born astronaut. According to the Steelers, more than six million towels have passed into the population. "I think every great nation has a flag," Pittsburgh safety Troy Polamalu said. "I think the Steeler Nation, it's obvious that that's our flag."

## Business example: Livestrong bracelets

An excellent example of a nonprofit using symbolism is Lance Armstrong's Livestrong Foundation, formerly the Lance Armstrong Foundation, and its creation of the Livestrong bracelets that continue to be ubiquitous today. Armstrong, after his testicular cancer diagnosis, started a foundation to raise awareness about, and funds for, cancer research. In 2004, his foundation hired Milkshake Media to help redesign a small portion of its Web site, the online resource center for cancer survivors. As a result of interviews with cancer survivors, Katherine Jones, founder of Milkshake Media, says that something unexpected happened. "We thought they wanted medical resources," Jones told *Fast Company* magazine. "[Instead] they wanted to talk about how cancer had changed their lives emotionally, physically, and practically." She suggested creating a distinct brand for this passionate community. Jones found inspiration in Armstrong's memoir, *It's Not About the Bike: My Journey Back to Life*, where she found this line: "All I wanted to do was tell people to fight like hell." Jones morphed Armstrong's gritty attitude and a play on his name and created the name "Livestrong." Focus groups were split on the name, as no one in the cancer community was using such defiant language, but Armstrong was not afraid. "HE LOVED IT," a foundation staffer e-mailed Jones's team.

Nike came on board as well. Usually the company wouldn't involve themselves with its athletes' foundations, but when executives heard about Livestrong, they immediately thought of the rubber bracelets they were testing on athletes. Nike offered to make five million emblazoned with "Livestrong" but instead of orange, it suggested yellow, the color of Armstrong's Tour de France jersey. Armstrong and then-girlfriend Sheryl Crow wore the symbols during the Tour de France in 2004 and presidential candidate John Kerry, a prostate cancer survivor himself, started wearing one. According to Kat Jones, Armstrong's *Oprah* appearance shut down Yahoo!'s servers when watchers tried to buy the bracelets. At its peak, the foundation, which hadn't sold anything prior to the wristbands, was selling one hundred thousand a day. In less than two years, annual revenue shot up from $15 million to $40 million. "When I heard that Nike was making five million of them, I was a little skeptical," Armstrong said. "I figured we'd be shooting them at each other for years."

Even today, as Armstrong has become embroiled in racing controversy and resigned from the organization, his significant contributions to cancer awareness and research and the success of the bracelets seem to remain unaffected by his infamy. According to Livestrong executives, donations increased 7 percent after August 23, 2012, when the U.S. Anti-Doping Agency announced it would strip Armstrong of his seven titles in the Tour de France. Donations went up 15 percent after mid-October 2012, when USADA released a mammoth file of evidence that showed Armstrong used banned drugs and blood transfusions throughout his cycling career. The charity also says only eight donors have asked for refunds in the wake of the scandal. It

seems people are more loyal to the cause the bracelets symbol-
ize than to the man behind it.

Livestrong—the brand the foundation didn't even set out to
create—could help it avoid a similar fate. By 2009, the foundation adopted the name that its supporters had already been using for some time. Livestrong is the rare example, Jones said, of
a parent brand being overtaken by an offshoot.

It is this brand offshoot that has enabled Livestrong to continue to be a force in cancer awareness and research, and the
ubiquitous bracelets continue to be a symbol for what they have
achieved. According to the Livestrong Foundation, over eighty
million bracelets have been sold to date. And it doesn't look like
those bracelets are going anywhere for a long time to come.

||||||||||||||||||

The key to shared symbols, like the Terrible Towel and the
Livestrong bracelet, is not the symbol itself. What is important
is how the meaning of the symbols binds a community together.
People who are part of the community truly understand its
meaning and are moved by it. For Steelers fans, we wave the
Towel to rally our players when they need our help to accomplish a crucial first down. No matter that the players are on TV
and they can't hear or see us. We know they can feel us. Yes, I
know that may seem ridiculous to non-fans, but die-hard fans
understand the power of the Towel. Cancer patients wear the
Livestrong bracelet because it reminds them of the "fight like
hell" attitude of Lance Armstrong, and it links them to others
around the world who wear it in support of their loved ones

who are fighting the disease, too. It reminds them daily that they can beat cancer. There is also something about the power of the symbol to make people feel special and unique. In the next chapter we'll take a look at how powerful it can be to make customers or fans feel this way by doing what Gaga does so well—make them feel like rock stars.

# Make Them Feel like Rock Stars

"Dear Mama Monster,

My name is Erika. You pulled me up on stage twice during the Born This Way Ball in Australia. First in Sydney, and again in Perth. First of all I want to thank you for that opportunity. You have no idea what I went through just to get to go to your shows. I saved up so much money and sold my entire wardrobe except for my school uniform and my work uniform and I worked two jobs while completing my final year at school. I worked for 6 months on a different costume for each show so thank you for noticing me and giving me the opportunity to stand with you and show everybody how brave I really am.

**Love from Erika.@erikamayowens"**

Since the dawn of the advertising age, brands have always been the marketing stars. The product or service or company was the center of attention in advertising. Companies controlled the branding message and spread it broadcast-style on the three television networks. Fast-forward to our social-media-drenched world, a world in which everyone has a cell phone in his or her pocket that is a content-creating machine. Ordinary people using technology can send photos and messages about products and brands to a worldwide audience via Twitter, Facebook, and YouTube. The customers are now the stars. Smart companies, in a bid to keep their business, are making customers feel special by shining a spotlight on them. It helps cement the existing bond with the company. When companies go over the top to make customers feel special, the customers can't help but talk about it with all of their friends and family.

Gaga, an actual rock star, makes her own fans feel like rock stars themselves. Throughout this book, I have discussed Gaga's love for and loyalty to her fans. She is humble enough to understand that she would not be where she is without their support. She may be the Queen of Pop, but she does so many things that make her fans feel like royalty—things like sending tired and hungry fans pizza while they wait in line overnight for an album signing or stopping the tour bus and inviting fans in for tea and a chat. Here are some more key ways Gaga shows that she is a fan of her fans.

## Phone a Monster

Gaga instituted a tradition during the Monster Ball Tour where she calls a fan in the audience. She tells the audience that she's going to call one of them right then—during the concert. She dials the phone and the sound of the phone ringing fills the arena. "I hope they're not busy," she says to laughter in the crowd. "Hello?" says a tentative fan on the other end of the line. "Hello, it's Lady Gaga." Immediately the fan is brought up live on one of the giant video screens talking on the phone with Gaga for everyone to see and hear. At this point, the fan usually starts screaming, "I love you!" Gaga compliments them on what they are wearing and asks if they would like to come backstage after the show and have a drink. Of course this elicits more screaming, but this time from everyone in the arena who wishes it were they who were being asked backstage.

What's so great about this ritual is the way it's designed. Gaga's team has picked the person ahead of time and is ready with a phone and a video camera operator. Usually when you go to a concert, all the action is happening up on stage. But in this example, Gaga brings a random fan in a massive crowd into the spotlight. Then Gaga says to the fan, "I'm sending up some people who are going to bring you and your friends down to the front of the stage so you can have a better view of the concert."

For a Little Monster, this is life-changing. You can just imagine what this fan is experiencing. Their idol has just spoken to them on the phone, complimented them, gotten them a seat in front of the stage, and given them a backstage pass. It doesn't get any better than this for a superfan. This is something they will tell everyone they know. Even the fans that just saw this happen will relay the experience to other fans.

Another great aspect of Phone a Monster is that Lady Gaga partnered with Virgin Mobile to make it happen. Before calling the fan, she tells the audience that Virgin is supporting the Monster Ball Tour to raise money to help homeless youth by donating $20,000 each time she calls a fan. In some cities on the tour, fans that volunteered their time at homeless youth organizations were offered VIP concert tickets courtesy of Virgin. Gaga explains to the audience that this campaign is important to her because there is such a high rate of homelessness among LGBT youth, as some parents kick kids out when they find out the children are gay. This partnership was part of Virgin's Freefest campaign, which raised $500,000 along with seventy-five thousand hours of community service for various charities such as the National Alliance to End Homelessness (NAEH). The partnership keeps Gaga fans talking and perhaps new fans are made when Virgin's customers find out about it.

## Give Them Keys to the Ball

Gaga came up with a new tradition for the Born This Way Ball, her 2012–13 tour. She is giving away a "Monster Pit Key" to the first fan waiting in line at each of the 110 tour shows. Before the tour started, Gaga tweeted a picture of a necklace with a metal skull and ponytail (reminiscent of the symbol discussed in the last chapter). Gaga says, "This is a necklace I'll give to the first monster in line every night at the Ball. It's a symbol of the 'key' that opens the pit every night." The Monster Pit is an enclosed general admission area around the stage reserved for hard-core fans. She's keeping the real key, a much larger cardboard version, for herself, though (see Fig. 6.1). In a follow-up tweet, she elaborated: "The real monster pit key will be signed by this fan and returned to me. There'll be 110 necklaces & signatures Mar. 2013."

Gaga has been posting pictures of the Monster Pit Key holders from each concert to her Littlemonsters.com profile. She's turned these super die-hard fans into rock stars. All the One Percenters in the Little Monsters community get to see that one fan out of tens of thousands at each concert is singled out for this honor. The fact that Gaga has the fan sign the real key that she then keeps is extra special. The fans usually clamor for her autograph, but instead, she is the one asking for theirs. The Monster Pit Key holders also get to go backstage and meet Gaga, and this is where they sign the key. They then post the

**Fig. 6.1** Little Monster Gary Sim poses with the Monster Pit Key from the Singapore stop of the Born This Way Ball Tour on May 29, 2012 *(courtesy of Gary Sim)*

photos of themselves backstage on their Littlemonsters.com profile pages. There's nothing new about artists bringing fans backstage. But what Gaga has done is ritualize the process by rewarding the die-hard fans for their dedication and showcasing them for the rest of the community. She makes them rock stars in their own right.

## Be Like Bruce

Bruce Springsteen is known for pulling fans up on stage to dance. Remember Courtney Cox immortalized as the fan that Bruce picked to come on stage in the "Dancing in the Dark" video? This is the ultimate rock-star moment for a fan. Gaga does something similar in the Born This Way Ball but makes it her own by ritualizing it. During the last song of the concert, "Marry the Night," Gaga picks a young fan from one of the front rows. He or she appears to be around eleven or twelve years old and becomes part of a narrative she is weaving right before the song starts. She asks the fan his or her name and introduces him or her to the crowd. She holds the fan's hand and walks down to the end of a runway in the middle of the general admission seats. Still holding the fan's hand, she tells this story to the audience: "When I was your age, I used to lay in bed at night and I would dream that if I played piano enough every day, and if I practiced, and if I really really put time into it, I would someday be a star. I used to perform outside and there would be maybe 3 people at the show. And then I'd perform at bars and there'd be like 30 people. Then there were 300. And then 3,000." She is now standing directly behind the fan. She puts her hands over the eyes of the fan and says slowly, "Then one day . . . ," and removes her hands from the fan's eyes, "there were . . . Thirty. Thousand. People." As people erupt in cheers and applause, Gaga says, "It could be you. It could be anyone in this world." She looks at the fan onstage and says, "It could be you." She continues, "There's no dream that's too big. And I know that because I get to look in the face of 30,000 dreams every night." The slow strains of "Marry the Night" begin and Gaga serenades the fan. As the high energy beats of the pounding anthem to New York City kick in, Gaga starts jumping up and down, encouraging the crowd to jump as well, all the while still holding the young fan's hand. She has, in essence, taken a fan and shown him or her what she experiences on stage and narrated the whole thing. The fan has literally become the star. This is a night that young fan will never forget—standing next to his or her idol in front of thirty thousand people. In fact, it's a night that those thirty thousand people won't soon forget either.

## Spotlight Gifts

Another way Gaga makes fans feel like rock stars is to highlight their gifts. Little Monsters are very creative and are constantly making Gaga-themed art, often incorporating the shared symbols of the community. They pour their passion and creativity into making something they think the singer will like that also will impress their fellow monsters. Gaga has turned this into a ritual at the Born This Way Ball. During a break in the show, she and two dancers sit at the edge of the stage in front of the Monster Pit. Fans come to the Ball bearing gifts that they throw to Gaga, who opens them onstage. At the Brisbane, Australia, stop of the tour, Gaga received a black vest with "Born This

Way" painted on the back, a giant mechanical monster paw that glowed red when turned on, and a locked box with personal notes from a gaggle of fans. For each gift she really likes, she asks that fan to come backstage. The show is loud and over-the-top, but this moment is very intimate as she converses one-on-one with the gift-giving fans in front of thirty thousand others.

## Recognize Standouts Using Social Media

The existence of fan art is an indication of really engaged fans. Only One Percenters are going to spend their time drawing something or creating an art piece to show their passion for the brand. Little Monsters know that, besides the front row at concerts, Littlemonsters.com is the place to go to show off your fan art to Mother Monster. The front page of Littlemonsters.com resembles Pinterest in that it is a scrolling visual feed of images. Much of it is artwork created by fans. One day Gaga will leave her hotel in a flowing white strapless dress and tiara, and the next day fan drawings of Gaga in the dress will be posted to the site. Gaga seems to be on the site almost daily, commenting on and liking the fan art she fancies. She also posts links to the fan art on her Facebook and Twitter accounts. To have your art tweeted out to thirty million people by Gaga is a rock-star moment for sure.

For one artist, her Little Monster dream came true. Twenty-year-old Helen Green from England had been posting renderings of Gaga on her Littlemonsters.com profile for five months. One particular drawing was of a poster for a fictional Disney movie called *Born This Way*, with Gaga drawn as a princess with her paw up. Gaga saw the drawing and tweeted a link to it, saying, "This is my favorite thing in life. Just putting it out there Disney can we make this happen?" Helen was able to meet Gaga backstage at the Born This Way Ball stop in Twickenham, England. The two hit it off and Gaga took to Littlemonsters.com to announce some news—she had hired Helen to be a part of the creative team in the Haus of Gaga:

LADIES, GENTLEMEN,
MONSTERS, AND PRINCESS HIGHs
PLEASE Welcome Helen Green to the Haus of Gaga,
The first Little Monsters [*sic*] to be inducted into our
factory of fame. She is one of the more talented young fine
artists we've seen in a while.

All my love, i told you you were
superstars, LG

Helen posted a comment to Gaga's post:

This is so incredible, I'm struggling to find words right now. To have my work recognised by Gaga in person meant everything to me. To be welcomed as the first Little Monster to the Haus of Gaga is truly phenomenal, I didn't think that was even possible. This couldn't happen without the Little Monster community, thank you so much for sharing my work and supporting me.

The Little Monsters community went nuts. One of their own had just been inducted into Gaga's inner circle. Everyone was so happy for Helen, congratulating her on her work. Gaga had made this young artist into a rock star in the community.

For businesses, the objective is to put the spotlight on your customers and highlight them to the larger community. It could be a small gesture or it could be something that rocks their world and elevates their standing in your customer community. Here are a few ideas from other businesses to get you thinking.

## Business example: Ant's Eye View

Ant's Eye View is a boutique social-business consulting firm with offices in Seattle, San Jose, and Austin. (Disclosure: I worked for Ant's Eye View during the event I am about to describe. Also, as of this writing, they have just been acquired by PricewaterhouseCoopers.) Ant's Eye View is a young company (just four years old) but is filled with experienced social-business practitioners from some of the top companies in the country, including Microsoft, Dell, Apple, IBM, Intuit, LEGO, and Electronic Arts. The Ants, as they call themselves, help their Fortune 1000 clients become more customer-focused by engaging with their own customers in social media. They teach their clients that businesses don't just create customers, but that their purpose should be to create customers who create customers. That is, have a business that is worth talking about. Much of Ant's Eye View's business comes in the form of referrals. They deliver solid social-business strategies and they also know how to make a client feel like a rock star by having a little fun when he comes to town.

That client is Rod Brooks, the chief marketing officer for PEMCO Insurance. In May 2010, Rod was flying to Austin for a conference, arriving late after a long flight from Seattle. He was only going to be in Austin for thirty-six hours, but Ant's Eye View wanted the visit to be memorable. Many companies would have just taken their client out for drinks or dinner, but the Ants wanted to do something bigger. They hired a service called Celeb 4 a Day, a firm that dispatches paparazzi to turn someone into a celebrity. As Rod descended the escalator into the baggage-claim area, he was surrounded by photographers that began snapping pictures and shouting questions to him. Because of all the commotion, surprised tourists began pointing and whispering, "Who is that guy?" Rod related the incident on his Facebook page:

> Then, complete strangers and fellow travelers got out THEIR CAMERAS and started taking my picture. There was talk of autographs! By this time, I was playing along with the gag. It was a really great greeting. Out the door and into the parking lot we went. The pictures were still flashing away and traffic in the parking lot was slowing down and taking it all in.

Sean McDonald, SVP and managing director of Ant's Eye View's Austin office, says about the idea of turning his client into a rock star:

**Fig. 6.2** Ant's Eye View gives their client PEMCO CMO Rod Brooks the star treatment *(Sean McDonald)*

The outcome was spectacular because Rod is such a great sport and enjoys people (even at 11:15 p.m. in the Austin airport). During the [conference], I heard Rod retell his memorable experience of his celebrity reception in Austin. Rod got a ride to his hotel after answering all the paparazzi questions and being photographed over 100 times in 15 minutes. [Ant's Eye View] got the opportunity to not only thank a customer, but to celebrate a customer with some fun memories, pictures, and a story that gets retold over and over again.

Rod's celebrity moment was made into a magazine cover, complete with his image and quotes (see Fig. 6.2).

Even a small gesture can make your customers know you appreciate them. Make it creative and give your customers something to talk about.

## Business example: Chevrolet

Chevrolet created the Chevy Ignites program to highlight customers who loved the car brand. Spike Jones, the former senior vice president of customer experience and digital/word of mouth at Fleishman-Hillard, helped devise the program. Says Jones, "The seed of the concept is . . . [for the brand to] become fans of our fans and shine the huge spotlight of Chevy on them."

Chevy and Fleishman-Hillard looked for people who were fans, had good stories, and didn't have a large social presence. They approached them at events or via e-mail and then followed up with a phone call. Once they connected, the fans were sent a metal die-cut card that sent them to a secret URL with a personalized number and password on it. The sleeve of the card said "We've been waiting for you."

Once at the site, fans could choose a limited edition T-shirt (that had no Chevy branding on it but did have the logo of the Chevy Ignites program incorporated into the designs). Fans could then share their stories, interact with others, and keep up-to-date for events in their area.

Chevy found Jared Gaff, a Dallas, Texas, resident and Irish immigrant who had a passion for graphic design and muscle cars. Fleishman-Hillard spent a day with him at his home in Dallas with a camera crew and asked him to talk about his passions. Jones explains, "We didn't give him a script or prompt him to talk about anything. He could talk about anything, so he talked about how he got into graphic design . . . and how he saved up his money to buy his dream car—the brand new Camaro SS.

"We packaged the video back up and gave it to him and said, 'Thanks so much for your time' and walked away. We didn't post it on any Chevy properties at all." Gaff, on the other hand, immediately took the video to the auto message boards and talked about his experience of making the video. The video got thirteen thousand views on YouTube, and Jared became the most influential person on Twitter for the subject of Camaros.

Chevy made Jared Gaff feel like a celebrity, starring in his own personal mini-documentary. And they gave him something to talk about with others.

## Business example: eBay

Online auction site eBay has long understood that its customers, the sellers, are the heart of its business. In 2002, eBay kicked off the first ever eBay Live! event in Anaheim, California. This was a three-day annual conference for eBay users to gather together to talk about all things eBay, and, in particular, how to leverage eBay as a business tool. "It was an event whose time had come," said Tom Cotton, one of the coordinators of eBay Live! "The idea for eBay Live was born out of a desire to really celebrate the community of buyers and sellers who are the heart and soul of this company. We've been amazingly successful working together in the 'virtual' world, but we felt it was time. We wanted to bring the people who make up eBay, buyers, sellers and staff, together face-to-face." That first event exceeded eBay's expectations with over 5,600 attendees from nineteen different countries. "Most companies are defined by their products, their executives, and their financial goals," eBay CEO Meg Whitman told attendees at that first event. "Not eBay . . . eBay is defined by you."

At its peak, eBay Live! attracted some fifteen thousand attendees. One feature of the conference was designed to literally make customers feel like celebrities. To enter the conference hall for the opening night gala dinner, where CEO Whitman and other executives would address the attendees, customers walked down a red carpet through a gauntlet of eight hundred cheering eBay employees wearing light-blue shirts. There was also a cameraman at the start of the gauntlet, projecting customers up on the giant screen outside the hall, à la an awards show. Customers were "blown away . . . eyes welled up with tears," as one person commented on an eBay forum, describing the event. Being treated like a rock star by a company they patronized made a huge impact. One eBay seller uploaded a video he had recorded of the 2008 eBay Live! event to YouTube and in the video description shared his feeling:

> This was one of those great moments in my life I will never forget! Ebay treated me like a King at the 2008 Ebay Live Gala at Chicago's McCormick Place. Ebay treated me better in one weekend, then the 14 years I have been with my day job (Time to work for Ebay full time). All 800 employees greeted the attendees on a red carpet and cheered attendees on (Wow! I felt like a rock star!!!).

As a side note, eBay Live! was discontinued in 2010 due to its unwieldy size. eBay replaced it with multiple smaller events around the country. They have been partnering with local eBay sellers' groups to put on the events, and in some cities they have re-created the red-carpet treatment.

||||||||||||||||||||

Making your customers feel like rock stars is something they won't soon forget. As the eBay customer above said, we are often taken for granted by our bosses and maybe by our own families. When someone or something makes us feel special, and singles us out for recognition, it fosters an emotional connection. It's a feeling we will tell others about for a long time. Gaga, Ant's Eye View, Chevy, and eBay came up with creative ways to treat their customers like rock stars that gave their customers reasons to gush about them. Now let's explore how Gaga keeps her Little Monsters, and the rest of us, gushing and buzzing about almost everything she does.

# Generate Something to Talk About

"When you make music or write or create, it's really your job to have mind-blowing, irresponsible, condomless sex with whatever idea it is you're writing about at the time."

— **Lady Gaga**

Translation of the prior Gaga-speak: Don't play it safe when it comes to your work. No one talks about products or companies that are just average. The way Gaga sees it, whatever you are working on, you should blow it out. Go big or go home. Create something remarkable. The lesson here is to create word of mouth with your One Percenters by giving them something to talk about. Your most passionate fans love to talk about you but you need to make sure they always have something to talk about. The key here is standing out, doing something remarkable so that people will remark on it. You have to create a "purple cow," as my friend Seth Godin illustrated in his best-selling book of the same name. A purple cow will stand out in a herd of brown cows, and people will talk about it. In this chapter, I will show you Gaga's approach to generating things for her Little Monsters to talk about as well as some of her more famous examples. I'll also show you how two businesses are getting their One Percenters talking.

Lady Gaga is a pro at generating word of mouth and getting people buzzing. She is a performance artist at heart and isn't afraid of taking risks. But the real genius lies in what is behind the shock value of her antics. Each over-the-top idea is rooted in a message with corresponding symbolism. Gaga believes that if you are going to do something, do something mind-blowing. Do it big. Stand for something and illustrate it through your art. Gaga explained to Anderson Cooper in a *60 Minutes* interview, "I'm a true academic when it comes to music and when it comes to my style, my fashion. There's nothing that I've ever put on my body that I didn't understand where it came from, the reference of it, who inspired it. There's always some sort of a story or a concept that I'm telling." In a way, she is directing her antics to her Little Monsters while also getting those outside the inner circle talking. While the media and casual observers might not always pick up on the nuanced messaging behind her crazy outfits or stunts, Little Monsters will dissect and debate what things mean on online fan forums, Twitter, and Littlemonsters.com. Often Gaga will chime in on the conversation to help them understand. This helps bind the fan community together because they "get" her, even if outsiders do not. But it also keeps the outsiders talking, wondering, and attempting to interpret. Fans are inspired by how Gaga pushes boundaries with her artistry and feel proud to be part of a trendsetter's community:

You know, I feel so so happy to be Gaga's fan and not a fan of basic artists. I realise that Gaga will always be like this: INNOVATIVE. And that makes me proud of her forever. It does give me hope for her wonderful future as an artist. She tries to innovate and be original, in everything, not only in music, but also in fashion, social media and show concepts. SIMPLY AMAZING GIRL—A LEGEND

— Fan comment from user "BestStatus" on a GagaDaily.com forum

Here are three buzz-building examples of how Gaga has gotten people talking.

## The Meat Dress

"I never thought I'd be asking Cher to hold my meat purse." This was the first thing Gaga said onstage as she accepted the award for Video of the Year for "Bad Romance" from Cher at the 2010 MTV Video Music Awards. She would end up with eight awards before the night was over, tying a record for the second highest number of wins in one night. But it wasn't the eight awards that people were talking about. What had the audience abuzz was Gaga's dress, shoes, hair ornament, and purse made entirely of raw meat. She was a spectacle on stage in her red flank-steak ensemble.

After the show, the media response was loud and varied. PETA denounced the dress, saying that "wearing a dress made from cuts of dead cows is offensive enough to bring comment, but someone should whisper in her ear that more people are upset by butchery than are impressed by it." Vegetarian singer

Morrissey had no problem with the dress as long as it was a social or political statement, and not just a "loony idea." *Time* magazine went on to name the outfit the "Top Fashion Statement of 2010." Even fearless fashion experimenter Cher was impressed, tweeting "Meat purse was genius! . . . As Art piece [the dress] was astonishing."

As Morrissey had correctly surmised, there was more to the dress than just cow couture. Gaga, a longtime supporter of gay rights, was using the dress to draw attention to the possible repeal of the "Don't Ask, Don't Tell" policy of the U.S. military. This policy barred openly gay, lesbian, or bisexual people from military service. She had previously spoken out on DADT in a speech for the National Equality March in Washington DC in October 2009. A few months before the MTV awards show, in May 2010, the U.S. House of Representatives approved the Murphy amendment to the National Defense Authorization Act, which would provide for the repeal of DADT. Now it was up to the Senate to take a vote on the repeal. Gaga was out to put pressure on Senate Majority Leader Harry Reid to take up this vote. She was going to use the MTV awards to make a statement. And a statement she made.

In a Renaissance-inspired red and gold Alexander McQueen gown and gold feather headpiece, she walked the award show's white carpet with four military veterans who were part of the Servicemembers Legal Defense Network, a group that opposed DADT. Gaga told MTV's Sway on the white carpet, "These soldiers that are with me today have all been discharged from the air force or army, or opted to leave on their own. . . . Their stories are truly inspiring, and in my opinion—and as so many young people around the world believe—'don't ask, don't tell' is wrong, it's sick, it's immoral." Gaga paid for the veterans to fly to the event and procured prime seats for them in the row behind her at the Los Angeles Nokia Center.

Near the end of the show, Gaga changed into the now famous meat dress, which got mainstream media attention as she won the biggest award of the night, Video of the Year. The idea behind the dress was to illustrate that underneath all of our skin colors, religions, and beliefs, we are all made of flesh and bone. "It is a devastation to me that I know my fans who are gay . . . feel like they have governmental oppression on them. That's actually why I wore the meat tonight," Gaga explained in an interview with Ellen DeGeneres filmed right after the MTV show. Still dressed in the now-smelly meat dress, Gaga said, "If we don't stand up for what we believe in and if we don't fight for our rights, pretty soon we're going to have as much rights as the meat on our own bones."

That night Gaga tweeted to her six-million-strong Twitter army, a photo of herself with her military entourage: "Gay Veterans were my VMA dates. Repeal Don't Ask Don't Tell. CALL HARRY REID to Schedule Senate Vote." Reid tweeted back to Gaga that he had already scheduled a vote for the following week.

Later in 2010, the Senate finally passed the repeal and President Obama signed the repeal into law on December 22, 2010. Now I'm not insinuating that the meat dress was the catalyst behind the repeal, but Gaga did get the world talking and ingeniously turned a dress made out of steak into a symbol for gay rights. She put her meat dress where her mouth was and took a stand on an issue important to her and the gay community. She rallied the Little Monsters to take action and try to change this discriminatory law.

The meat dress continues to be talked about. After the MTV awards show, Gaga had the dress dried, preserved, and painted to restore its original raw-meat color. In September 2012, the Rock and Roll Hall of Fame opened a national tour about pioneering women in rock and roll, highlighting the evolution of women artists and their impact on music. Curator Meredith Rutledge-Borger told the Associated Press the exhibit, "Women Who Rock: Vision, Passion, Power" is inherently political, in part, as it highlights many "first ladies of rock" who have spoken loud and clear on women's rights, gay rights, and other issues through their music. Beyond the dress's shock value, Gaga's push for inclusion of gays or anyone else who is different helped cement her place as a pioneer, said Rutledge-Borger. "If you dig a little deeper, there's this important message of inclusion and family," she said. "That to me is really why she's so powerful."

## The Perfume

The list of music celebrities who have their own branded fragrance is a long one: Beyoncé, Jennifer Lopez, Christina Aguilera, Mariah Carey, Faith Hill, Rihanna, Taylor Swift, Katy Perry, Shakira, Gwen Stefani, and Britney Spears. Even Justin Bieber has a perfume. Actually he has two.

But Gaga, who notoriously does not go along with the crowd, was skeptical. She didn't want to have just another run-of-the-mill celebrity perfume. "I raised an eyebrow. I didn't really want to do it at first. But I wanted to create a fragrance that somebody who makes fragrances says, 'Well, how did they do that?'" Gaga explained to *Vogue* magazine.

In the first meeting Gaga had with executives from Coty, the perfume company that wanted to partner with her, she gave them her idea. The perfume, to be called Fame, must be black in the bottle, but when sprayed, become clear. She said, "It must smell enticing. You must want to lick and touch and feel it, but the look of it must terrify you."

Coty balked at first. Yael Tuil, vice president of Coty Beauty's global marketing department, recalls, "I was pregnant at that time. I started to sweat on my forehead [when I heard the idea]. I said, 'My God! That's impossible! How can we do that?'"

But given the chance to partner with the world's top pop superstar and create a perfume worth talking about, Coty decided to give it a try. They challenged their R&D scientists to fulfill Gaga's crazy vision. And the scientists came through. They invented an opaque-to-clear perfume technology that is now patent pending. Tuil gives props to Gaga for making them think outside the box, saying, "She was really behind the most important innovation in the fragrance industry in the last 20 years. She is really pushing boundaries."

The perfume is packaged in a sleek black box, which contains an egg-shaped bottle of black liquid topped with gold gilded monster claws. The back of the box spells out the ingredients: tears of belladonna, crushed heart of tiger *orchidea*, with a black veil of incense, pulverized apricot, and the combinative essences of saffron and honey drops.

The marketing campaign for Fame was as outside-the-box as the fragrance itself. Gaga admits she never expected Coty Beauty officials to approve her provocative black-and-white ads, which show her completely nude, with little men crawling over her body à la *Gulliver's Travels*. The strategically placed men look like little monsters. Literally.

Gaga said: "We [myself and photographer Steven Klein] thought, 'Let's just make the most epic fragrance campaign of all time and let's not care at all about whether they can even print it or show it on TV. Let's just do everything we ever dreamed of.' We basically did this purely for the pleasure of working together. We were just sort of sitting in the corner going, 'I can't believe they are letting us do this!'"

With six million bottles selling in the first week, it is the second-fastest selling fragrance after Chanel No. 5.

Renato Semerari, president of Coty Beauty, sums up Gaga's approach to whatever endeavor she is part of: "She is an artist that is never satisfied with the status quo—she always has this way of challenging everybody and trying to do something more, something different." This energy to continuously question the status quo and to have success after success doing it is what keeps people talking.

**Fig. 7.1 (opposite)** Lady Gaga arrives in a vessel to the 53rd Annual Grammy Awards in Los Angeles, California, February 13, 2011 *(Krista Kennell / Sipa / AP Photo)*

## The Vessel

"Lady Gaga is incubating. She is in an embryonic state and won't be born until the performance," a member of Gaga's entourage told press before the start of the 53rd Annual Grammy Awards in February 2011.

The press, fans, and televised audiences watched agape as a supine Lady Gaga, encased in a translucent egg-like contraption, was carried down the show's red carpet by four scantily clad male models dressed in nude tones. Kelly Osbourne, daughter of rocker Ozzy Osbourne, may have summed it up best as she watched the spectacle, tweeting "You will not believe your eyes when you see how @ladygaga showed up to the Grammys" (see Fig. 7.1).

Gaga was going to be performing the first single, "Born This Way," off her new album of the same name. The song was very different from most of the songs she had written on her first album, which were about clubbing, boys, and the dark aspects of fame. As Gaga later explained on *The Tonight Show* with Jay Leno, " 'Born This Way' is visually and thematically and lyrically about birthing a new race, birthing a race within the race of already existing cultures of humanity—that bears no prejudice and no judgment."

The lyrics to the song encourage people of all races and sexual orientations, as well as those who have been bullied or feel like outsiders, to be brave and believe in themselves.

When the song was released, it became the one thousandth No. 1 hit on *Billboard*'s Hot 100 chart. *Billboard* later said that in the fifty-two years of music charts, this was the first chart-topper to mention the word "transgendered." Gaga may not have set out to pen the next gay anthem, but that is what happened. Elton John said the song "will completely get rid of Gloria Gaynor's *I Will Survive*. This is the new *I Will Survive* . . . This is the new gay anthem. Actually, it's not a gay anthem—it can apply to anybody." Teenage Little Monsters also flocked to the song, saying online on Gaga fan forums that it had changed their lives and made them feel better about who they were. It gave them hope during times of depression and helped them feel brave about standing up to bullies and schoolmates who teased them.

Gaga explained her thoughts about writing the song:

I wanted to put my money exactly where my mouth is. The Little Monsters all over the world as well as the gay community have been tremendously supportive over the years and I have in turn been supportive . . . This is my chance to create something that is not only supportive of my political and social beliefs—not just for the gay community, but for everyone . . . This is also my chance to artistically say, 'I'm not being safe with this record.' I'm not trying to gain new fans. I love the fans I already have, and this is for them.

When it came time to introduce the song to the world, Gaga chose the worldwide stage of the Grammy Awards. She had already captivated everyone's attention before the show in the egg, or "vessel," as the designers, powerhouse fashion houses Hussein Chalayan and the House of Mugler, wanted it referred to. Then she set out to create an opening to her performance that would top it. As the first few strains of "Born This Way" began to fill the giant Staples Center in Los Angeles, Gaga was wheeled out on to the stage, now inside a larger version of the vessel. In a low-pitched voice, Gaga spoke the opening lines to the song, "It doesn't matter if you love him or capital H-I-M . . . Just put your paws up. . . . 'Cause you were born this way, baby . . ."

A top hatch in the vessel slid open. Gaga, dressed in a nude-colored latex ensemble, with microphone in hand, emerged singing. But Gaga looked different. Her hair was off-pink, flecked with something resembling amniotic remnants. Her cheekbones had morphed into little horns. Her shoulders sported bony protrusions. She looked reborn as part of some alien race.

"I was thinking about birth. I was thinking about embryos. Even my hair color was a washed-out rose color . . . it was meant to be a hair expression, an afterbirth," she explained to Jay Leno later. With her dancers around her in similar getups, they did look like a newly born alien race. Again, Gaga used a performance-art piece to convey a message that was important to her. We are all the same. Same DNA. We should treat each other with acceptance and love. She did this in a way that generated ideas and new things to ponder.

By the end of the night, Gaga had won three Grammys: Best Pop Vocal Album, Best Female Pop Vocal Performance, and Best Short Form Music Video for the song "Bad Romance." Gaga's take on the evening: "Not only did we take home some awards, which was an honor and a dream of mine since I was very, very young, but also because the message of 'Born This Way' is so positive and so much about self love and empowerment."

The next day, the egg was on the lips of her fans and the news media. It was talked about around the world. But what was also talked about was the new song and what it meant. Little Monsters immediately flocked to the song, tagging tweets with "#bornthisway." Gaga had used performance art not just to get attention for her new single but also to get people thinking about her vision of transforming the culture into a kinder, braver world where everyone is valued.

As Lady Gaga has shown us, it is the combination of generating a buzz and the meaning behind it that engages fans' imaginations and creativity. Buzz just for the sake of trying to get people talking will only go so far and will often die on the vine. But creating meaningful experiences in ways that catch people's attention has a much longer shelf life and has the ability to spark conversations between customers and create energy among them. As of this writing, Gaga already has people talking about her upcoming album *ARTPOP*, which doesn't even have a release date yet. Apparently it's not a regular album but a multimedia experience that will come in different forms. She announced to fans on Littlemonsters.com that one of the ways it will be released is through a mobile and computer application, or app, and is "completely interactive with chats, films for every song, extra music, content, gaga inspired games, fashion updates, magazines, and more still in the works!" She explained the reason for the format: "You inspired me to create something that communicated with images, because YOU do, YOU communicate with me and each other with .gifs and pictures, and artwork, graphics ALL DAY 24/7/ YOU'RE an ARTPOP generation. Im hoping you will all continue to grow together and stay connected through your creativity." It is an understatement to say those fans are excited. There are daily conversations on fan sites and Littlemonsters.com, all speculating on songs, collaborators, the app, and what exactly *ARTPOP* means. The album probably won't be out until spring 2013, but already it looks like Gaga has had "mind-blowing, irresponsible, condomless sex" with the album concept.

Two companies that understand this idea have created interactive customer experiences, and they get people talking. Innocent's yearly Big Knit for charity and FreshBooks RoadBurn offer the rare combination of giving customers something to talk about and making sure that that something is meaningful and engaging. How do you get your customers to rally behind a cause? Build in a word-of-mouth factor.

## Business example: Innocent

Innocent, the UK-based smoothie and juice company, offers a firsthand look at a successful campaign that creates meaningful buzz. The company donates 10 percent of its profits to charity. That in and of itself is meaningful. One way they do this that involves their customers and gives people something meaningful to rally around is their annual Big Knit. They ask customers to knit little hats for their juice and smoothie bottles that will be displayed for two weeks at large grocery stores every November. For every behatted bottle sold, Innocent donates twenty-five cents to Age UK, a charity that helps the elderly pay their heating bills over the harsh English winter. According to their Web site, "We first got our needles out nine years ago when we knitted 20,000 hats to raise £10,000 for Age Concern. Since then, the Big Knit has grown every year, and in 2011 we smashed the £1 million mark of total money raised over the campaign's history." In 2011, 1.5 million hats were sent in to the company.

Supporters are encouraged to start their own knitting circles to recruit their friends to the effort. Innocent provides all of the materials, including invitations, a hatometer to keep track of hats produced, as well as patterns and knitting instructions. Innocent also uses their Facebook page to have fans vote on "Hat of the Week." People can't resist buying one of the bottles that stand out on the store shelf in their warm, fuzzy toboggans (see Fig. 7.2). Could you?

As the Big Knit continues to grow, it's obvious that the power to create a buzz stems in large part from people's desire to make a difference in their communities and find meaningful work to do. The idea of knitting hats for smoothie bottles is creative and fun but would not have held the public's attention for long without the very real and meaningful charity work it serves to promote.

**Fig. 7.2** Examples of hats knitted by customers for Innocent's Big Knit Campaign *(Innocent)*

## Business example: FreshBooks

FreshBooks is a Toronto, Ontario–based company that provides cloud accounting and invoicing services to millions of users, helping them to send, receive, print, and pay invoices. In 2008, the company started the FreshBooks RoadBurn, a way to travel and meet up with customers where they live and work. Based on the assumption that a company should listen to its customers—really listen—the company decided to travel around in an RV emblazoned with the FreshBooks logo and have lunch or meetings with customers along the way. Dubbed RoadBurn, this buzz-generating idea took off. The company explains on the RoadBurn blog that "the FreshBooks Road-Burn may seem like a stunt or a marketing ploy but in reality it is pretty much what FreshBooks is all about . . . listening to its beautiful customer base and getting to know them on a level that other companies wouldn't make the effort to do so [sic]."

FreshBooks CEO Mike McDerment spoke with customer experience expert Becky Carroll about the first RoadBurn that happened on the way to the SXSW conference in Austin, Texas: "[Our three-person team] had eleven meals over a period of four days, meeting with more than a hundred customers over breakfast, lunch, and dinner." Besides asking questions of their customers, they encouraged the customers to network with each other. By the end of the meals, many of these customers were swapping business cards and planning to do business with one another. Saul Colt, former head of magic at FreshBooks, explains the word of mouth generated from RoadBurn. He says, "The buzz came from the fact that we met with some people as many as three times on our trip. That sort of effort gets people talking. We were first introduced to one of our customers in Miami at [the Future of Web Apps conference], then he joined us for lunch in his home town along our route and then we had dinner with him one night in Austin at SXSW. Creating real bonds with customers is something that people enjoy and talk about!" It is this ability to get customers talking—talking to one another, talking about FreshBooks and RoadBurn, and finding meaningful ways to engage with one another about the company's services that is the key to success for ideas like this. Saul says:

> Our goals for the trip were pretty simple. We wanted to meet as many customers as we could and create a real world relationship with the amazing customers who use our online service. Because we were meeting existing users, we did not look at this as a sales trip but rather an opportunity to listen. By meeting with and listening to our customers, we could not only refer them to other FreshBooks customers but we also learned a great deal about what it is they like (or LOVE) about FreshBooks and what they would like to see in future updates. I can't put into words how much this helps us.

Another way that RoadBurn was able to generate word of mouth was FreshBooks' use of social media and online discussions. According to Saul, they "were able to track people's interest on our trip by the large amount of chatter on blogs and most importantly Twitter . . . we followed all the comments about us and engaged in the conversation with these folks. As a result, even more people followed us and chatted about our trip!"

Perhaps Saul best describes the idea of generating something meaningful to talk about when he says: "Customers are always more than customers. They are people. Sure you can read that and think it's buzz speak or a cliché—but once you have shared a meal with someone and had a chat about stuff not revolving around work, you look at them differently and want to give them more then you already are. This isn't something I just learned on this trip, but the trip reconfirmed my belief of this."

Customers loved connecting with FreshBooks on the tour. Donna Vitan, a FreshBooks customer who followed the 2008 trip virtually through the RoadBurn blog, said: "It's clearly too bad that the trip was quite short! While I wasn't watching *The Hills*, I was hoping to get my reality fix from the adventures of FreshBooks." Joseph Crawford, a FreshBooks customer who participated in RoadBurn 2011, commented: "I was shocked when you came through Boston and held the dinner at Legal Seafood. It was a great time and was great to meet Mitch and everyone else."

||||||||||||||||||

Like Lady Gaga, Innocent and FreshBooks have found innovative, sophisticated, and creative ways to infuse their business and marketing plans with meaningful interactions and ways to engage customers and fans. What they all have in common is the belief that people always have energy to find meaning, create personal relationships, and talk to one another about what's important. Without meaning, generating buzz is a flash in the pan. Generating something to talk about that is meaningful and important ensures that your fans and customers will continue to look to you for inspiration and ideas.

## Building Monster Loyalty of Your Own

"I believe that everyone can do what I'm doing.
Everyone can access the parts of themselves that
are great. I'm just a girl from New York City who
decided to do this, after all. Rule the world!
What's life worth living if you don't rule it?"

— **Lady Gaga**

In Lady Gaga Land, nothing is impossible. A black perfume? Make it so, she says. Creating a business that engenders Monster Loyalty is not an overnight endeavor. But it most certainly can be done.

It takes a relentless focus on creating products and services that stand out and are worth talking about. It also requires a methodical cultivation of a company's One Percenters, the most passionate and engaged segment of the customer base. Lady Gaga's lessons outlined in the previous chapters provide a blueprint of sorts for finding and engaging the One Percenters. This chapter will help you think about how to apply Gaga's One Percenters strategies to your business.

## Focus on Your One Percenters

As detailed in chapter 2, the key to finding your most engaged customers is by creating vehicles for them to be part of. Help these passionate customers to self-identify. You may already have some engagement vehicles in place and not realize that this is where your One Percenters are contacting you.

The following is a list of some places to start to identify One Percenters:

- ♦ Referrals. Tracking where inbound inquiries came from will help you identify people who are spreading the word about you. Make sure your salespeople and online forms ask, "How did you hear about us?"

- ♦ Customer service touchpoints (1-800 number, Web forms, etc.). Research shows that for every one customer who complains to a company, there are twenty-five who don't. Those customers who take the time to contact a company do so for a reason. They may be frustrated but they want to get their problem solved. They may be one fix away from being an evangelist. Treat these customers with empathy when solving their problem. Go above and beyond to delight them.

- ♦ Incoming customer comments. Do you have customers who just contact you to give unsolicited feedback on making your business better? These folks feel such a connection to you that they want you to be better. Keep track of these concerned customers for further engagement.

- ♦ Frequent visitors to your stores. Can your store managers and employees identify frequent shoppers who love to shop with you and chat up employees?

♦ Opt-in e-mail newsletters. How many people are on your company's opt-in marketing lists?

♦ Third-party forums and blogs. Have you scanned the Web with listening tools, such as Radian6, to identify evangelists of your brand on third-party forums and blogs?

♦ Company-owned blog comment section. Are people frequently leaving comments on your company's blogs?

♦ Web content creators. Do you have any people who have created content only about your brand? Are there any fan Web sites, Tumblr sites, or Facebook pages for your brand? Are there customer-created YouTube videos about you?

♦ Subscribers to your social channels. Of course, people who subscribe to hear from you on your corporate social tools, such as Twitter, Facebook, YouTube, blogs, etcetera, are candidates to be One Percenters.

Once you identify where possible One Percenters reside, you can begin the strategic work of engaging them. The following pages present Gaga's loyalty lessons along with a set of questions and ideas on how you can begin to apply the lessons to your business.

## LESSON 2:

# Lead with Values

Gaga stands out from her musician contemporaries by standing for something bigger than herself and for sharing her values. She is a supporter of the gay community, fighting for marriage equality and repeal of the military's discriminating policy of "Don't Ask, Don't Tell." In turn, the gay community has been very loyal to Gaga because they feel she has been loyal to them. She also champions those in society who feel marginalized and are bullied for being different. In her song "Born This Way," she tells them to love who they are and to be brave. Her Born This Way Foundation is a movement for creating a kinder, more accepting world.

Customers feel a deep emotional connection with you when they identity with your values or cause. This kind of connection is not easy to engender but when it is done with integrity and commitment, customers will be very loyal to you. They will evangelize you to others and recruit new believers into the fold.

In thinking about how you can lead with values in your business, consider these two options:

◆ Is there a charitable cause that your company believes in? Is this the same cause that some segment of your customer base also believes in? Step up and show customers that you believe what they believe. Volunteer your company's resources to support the cause.

♦ Instead of just selling products, sell a dream. A vision. Think bigger about what would improve customers' lives or change their world. Challenge yourself and your organization to think big and create a message of inspiration for your industry.

LESSON 3:

## Build Community

Gaga first built her audience by playing gay clubs in New York City and embracing the LGBT community. Fiskars tapped into the scrapbooking community by building the Fiskateers program to serve them. Find the community that is already building around your product or company or tap into a community that is most likely to embrace you.

Here are some things to consider when thinking about community building:

♦ Are customers calling you to ask how they can meet other customers like themselves?

♦ Are customers already connecting to one another without you via the Web or social media?

♦ Ask customers to help develop a community program. Solicit their input and watch for the individuals who are eager to help. Can you appoint one as a leader of a specific program in your community-building efforts?

♦ Can you hold a fun event to bring customers together to swap stories with other customers, like the Fiskateers' Fiskafriendzy events?

♦ Add community features, such as online forums, to your Web site.

♦ Create and moderate an e-mail discussion group to get customers to connect.

♦ Start a blog to facilitate a conversation with your customers.

♦ Feature your current evangelistic customers in your marketing communications efforts. Solicit testimonials and sprinkle them liberally throughout your Web site, brochures, and advertising. Showcase to customers other customers who they will feel are just like them.

## LESSON 4:

## Give Fans a Name

Giving fans and customers a name, like Little Monsters or Maker's Mark Ambassadors, helps them identify as part of a like-minded community. It gives customers a moniker by which they can find other members of the community and connect.

There are a few ways to create this name:

♦ Find the name in the wild. Customers may already be referring to themselves with a name. Use online search or listening tools to find out how customers may be talking about themselves. The name they are using might be terrific!

♦ Come up with the name yourself. If you are creating a community or loyalty program and there isn't an existing name, or one that you like, you will need to create one yourself. Put your most creative folks, including agency partners, in a room and brainstorm.

♦ Have customers create the name with you. If you are open to including customers in the process, find some of your One Percenters and ask their opinion. Use an online survey or have an in-person facilitated meeting. Have your customers brainstorm alongside your own employees and jointly develop the name. Customers will love being part of the process and will feel ownership of the name.

LESSON 5:

## Embrace Shared Symbols

Gaga's Little Monsters have many shared symbols that everyone in the community understands. The shared knowledge and use of the symbols helps people bond. The claw hand is the best example of this. Only Little Monsters know to put one's claw hand up when they hear the call "Paws up!"

Here are some things to consider when applying this lesson to your business:

♦ For the symbols you create, watch how customers use or don't use them. Some symbols will resonate and some won't. Monitor customers' communications online and in social media to see if customers are referring to the symbol(s) or using them.

♦ Often customers will take a symbol you created and morph it to be something different.

♦ Customers will also create their own symbols. This happens often with consumer brands and the teenage fan culture. Millennials are very creative and tech savvy and can use computer programs to design sophisticated symbols connected with your brand.

♦ Be open to adopting symbols that fans have created or morphed out of your own. This gives them ownership and makes them feel that you are embracing them as part of your team.

## Make Them Feel Like Rock Stars

Gaga's lesson here is to become a fan of your fans. Celebrate your customers and put them in the spotlight. Make them feel special, like the rock stars that they are. Of course, you can't recognize everyone. You may only be highlighting 1 percent of the One Percenters, but this will make all customers feel that you value them.

Specific tactics to do this will vary by type of business, but here are a few things to consider:

♦ Find speaking engagements for your best customers to help them raise their profile in your industry.

♦ Feature your customers on your products, if applicable. For years, Jones Soda has featured a customer photo, submitted via their Web site, on each of their bottles.

♦ Invite select customers to special VIP events that give them access to something special, for example, a performance by a musician or group.

♦ Highlight a customer's success to the rest of the customer base—not just the success the customer is having with your product, but the overall success he or she is having with their business.

## Generate Something to Talk About

Lady Gaga understands standing out. As described in the chapter on this lesson, the ways in which she stands out often have a story behind them. She knows that by standing out, her story can be related through word of mouth by the One Percenters. The lesson here is to think about all aspects of your business and consider whether they are "word-of-mouth-worthy." That is, are the things you are doing worthy of a word-of-mouth comment or referral from a customer to someone else?

Here are some ideas to consider in making your business worth talking about:

♦ Understand your current customer recommendability and word of mouth. A terrific way to do this is to use the Net Promoter Score methodology developed by Fred Reichheld and Bain & Company. The methodology involves asking two questions to your current customer base: 1) "How likely is it that you would refer our company to a friend or colleague?" on a 0–10 scale with 10 being the highest and 2) an open-ended question asking customers to explain the score. In this second question, the Promoters (those respondents who answered 9 or 10) will tell you why they recommend you. This qualitative data is helpful in understanding the current word of mouth about you in your customer base.

♦ Use the word-of-mouth comments you learned about in question two of your Net Promoter study in your marketing communications efforts. Using similar phrasing in how customers already talk about you in your marketing efforts will help customers repeat those comments.

♦ Perform a customer touchpoint analysis to look at all places where your business interacts with customers. Touchpoints should include all human and physical interactions with customers, including your Web site, customer service contacts, physical stores, employees, receipts, invoices, social-media channels, telemarketing, proposals, e-mail signatures, brochures, and more. Look at each touchpoint and ask yourself if it is word-of-mouth-worthy. Is the interaction with a customer so remarkable that customers would make a comment about it to a friend, family member, or colleague?

♦ Design word of mouth into the product itself. Of course, we would all like to have groundbreaking products that stand out from the competition. But sometimes all it takes is including one design feature that gives people something to talk about.

In this book, we have examined how, in four short years, Lady Gaga has built an army of passionate fans that numbers in the tens of millions around the world. I've outlined her philosophy of how to build a customer base for the long term by focusing on her superfans, the One Percenters. I've broken down her strategies for creating loyalty and I used business examples to show you how the lessons apply to nonmusic businesses. Finally, in this chapter, I've asked you questions and given you ideas about how to apply Gaga's lessons to your business. I hope you have found Gaga's approach to loyalty as inspiring as it is to this marketer. Please let me know what you found interesting and applied to your business with success.

I believe Lady Gaga will be around for a very long time, which is one of the reasons I wanted to write this book. No doubt, she will continue to innovate in her business and inspire new legions of fans. There will be much to learn from her in the future and I hope to update this book throughout the years.

And if you can catch one of her live performances, by all means go. I promise you won't be disappointed. Paws up!

# ACKNOWLEDGMENTS

Gaga surrounds herself with talented, creative, and wicked-smart people who help make her vision a reality. She calls them the Haus of Gaga. For this book project, I gathered together a similar group of amazingly talented people. As we were working on the book, I jokingly called them the Haus of Huba. I loved working with them and highly recommend each of them: Todd Sattersten (agent/adviser), Kate Sage (editing/writing), Robyn Crummer-Olson (proofreading), Jason Reeves (creative), John Moore (adviser), Shelley Dolley (marketing), and Barbara Henricks, Margaret Kingsbury, Rusty Shelton and the team from Cave Henricks (publicity).

Thanks to Brooke Carey, Adrian Zackheim, Will Weisser, and Jackie Burke from Portfolio for supporting the book and bringing it to the world.

Thanks to those who shared their insights for the book, including Erin Nelson of Bazaarvoice, Spike Jones of WCG, and Dayle Hall of Aruba Networks. Thanks to Sean McDonald of Ant's Eye View and Rod Brooks of PEMCO for allowing me to tell their customer rock-star story. I want to acknowledge those who provided images and photos for the book, including Gary Sims, Joel Diaz, Sean McDonald, Jason Reeves, Simon Sinek, Innocent, Jim Stengel, and Susan Hickey of Millward Brown.

I also want to thank Keith Berlin and Stephanie Jax of dmg::events for their continued support and for helping me test the concepts in the book at their event. Thanks to Brad Fay of Keller Fay for his advocacy of this book and his fantastic launch idea. I especially want to thank Virginia Miracle and Jim Rudden of Spredfast for making the launch happen. Thanks to Suzanne Fanning and the folks at WOMMA for supporting the launch as well. Derrick Barry: Having you as part of the most fun keynote I have ever done for the book launch was amazing. Thank you. Thank you, Amy Neighbors, for your referrals and weekly encouragement during the writing of the book. Thanks to Jill Griffin for your assistance as well. Thanks to Sonya Reeves for pitching in when help was needed, even on the smallest things.

Thanks to the amazing folks at Czarnowski for being so great to work with over the past two years.

Thanks to my supportive friends who I didn't see much of for months while writing this book but who always had an encouraging word: Kelly Pierce, Charles Brown, Shelley Stewart Kronbergs, Annalisa Perez, Amy Swank, Robin Boesch, Heather Wiers, Stephen Graham, Walter Davis, Cameron Oefinger, Cody Edwards, Vu Doan, and Colton Wright.

Thanks to Jason, Sonya, and Emmett Reeves for being gracious and dealing with the many weeknights and weekends when I was holed up in my office, working on this book. Thanks to my family for your continued support.

And finally, thanks to Lady Gaga for being an inspiration—not just for the business world, but also for changing the world for the better.

# NOTES

**INTRODUCTION**

1. "Dear Mama Monster . . ." Bree Richards, fan letter to Gaga, Tumblr, accessed September 24, 2012, http://dear-mama-mon ster.tumblr.com/post/28833155687/dear-mama-mon ster-my-name-is-bree-richards-and-i.

3. Her achievements include . . . Keith Caulfield, "Lady Gaga Is *Billboard*'s 2010 Artist of the Year, Ke$ha Takes Top New Act," *Billboard*, December 9, 2010, http://www.billboard.com/ news/lady-gaga-is-billboard-s-2010-artist-of-1004134049 .story#/news/lady-gaga-is-billboard-s-2010-artist-of-10041 34049.story; "The 2010 *Time* 100," *Time*, accessed September 24, 2012, http://www.time.com/time/specials/packages/ completelist/0,29569,1984685,00.html; "Music's Top 40 Money Makers 2011," *Billboard*, February 11, 2011, http:// www.billboard.com/features/music-s-top-40-money-mak ers-2011-1005031152.story#/features/music-s-top-40-money- makers-2011-1005031152.story?page=5; Dorothy Pomerantz, "Lady Gaga Tops Celebrity 100 List," May 18, 2011, *Forbes*, http://www.forbes.com/2011/05/16/lady-gaga-tops-cele brity-100-11.html.

4. I started following her on . . . Lady Gaga's Facebook page, accessed September 24, 2012, http://www.facebook.com/

ladygaga; Lady Gaga's Twitter profile, accessed September 24, 2012, http://twitter.com/ladygaga.

5. **I first wrote about this** . . . Jackie Huba, "Loyalty Lessons from Lady Gaga," *Church of the Customer* (blog), February 23, 2010, http://www.churchofcustomer.com/2010/02/loyalty-lessons-from-lady-gaga.html.

5. **The largest consumer packaged-good companies** . . . Jonathon Mildenhall, Twitter post on Troy Carter visiting Coca-Cola, October 11, 2011, 8:04 a.m., http://twitter.com/ComeBeCreative.

5. **Technology companies like** . . . Lisa Pearson, "Engaging Your Superfans: Social Lessons from Lady Gaga's Manager," *Bazaarvoice:blog* (blog), June 25, 2012, http://www.bazaar voice.com/blog/2012/06/25/engaging-your-superfans-so cial-lessons-from-lady-gagas-manager.

## FROM STEFANI TO GAGA

9. **"When I wake up . . ."** "Lady Gaga Tells All: Rolling Stone's New Issue," *Rolling Stone*, June 21, 2010, http://www .rollingstone.com/music/news/lady-gaga-tells-all-roll ing-stones-new-issue-20100621.

12. **She began playing** . . . Vanessa Grigoriadis, "Growing Up Gaga," *New York* magazine, March 28, 2010, http://nymag .com/arts/popmusic/features/65127.

12. **"I was classically trained . . ."** Neil McCormick, "Lady Gaga: 'I've Always Been Famous, You Just Didn't Know It,'" *The Telegraph*, February 16, 2010, http://www.telegraph.co.uk/culture/music/rockandpopfeatures/7221051/Lady-Ga ga-Ive-always-been-famous-you-just-didnt-know-it.html.

12. **After an in-depth** . . . "Lady Gaga Interview—Howard Stern 2011," YouTube video, 1:19:21, from a performance on the *Howard Stern Show* on July 18, 2011, posted by "01world guy01," May 7, 2012, http://youtu.be/SwwT1viwA8M.

13. **She accompanied herself** . . . "Lady Gaga—The Edge of Glory on the Howard Stern Show!" YouTube video, from a performance on the *Howard Stern Show* on July 18, 2011, 5:25, posted by "Jonathon Mowery," May 8, 2012, http://youtu .be/0RS3XUEgWC0; Christian Blauvelt, "Lady Gaga Opens

Up to Howard Stern in Exhaustive 90-minute Interview, Performs Acoustic Version of 'The Edge of Glory'–Listen Here," *Entertainment Weekly*, July 18, 2011, http://music-mix.ew.com/2011/07/18/lady-gaga-how ard-stern-interview.

13. **"Wow. Helluva set of pipes . . ."** Melangie, July 20, 2011 (8:35 a.m.), comment on "Lady Gaga Does Acoustic on Howard Stern: Amazing or Expected?," *Celelbitchy* (blog), July 20, 2011, http://www.celebitchy.com/169643/lady_gaga_does_acoustic_on_ howard_stern_amazing_or_expected_/#comment-5250533.

13. **On a YouTube video . . .** "***ORIGINAL FULL VID*** Lady Gaga Sings at Park Hyatt Tokyo New York Bar," YouTube video, 3:41, posted by "MonkeySDLA," May 10, 2012, http:// youtu.be/OdCks_Nd1v0.

14. **"I left my entire family . . ."** Grigoriadis, "Growing Up Gaga."

14. **"Every day, when Stef . . ."** Lisa Rose, "Lady Gaga's Outrageous Persona born in Parsippany, New Jersey," *The Star-Ledger*, January 21, 2010, http://www.nj.com/entertainment/music/index.ssf/2010/01/lady_gaga_her_outrageous_perso.html.

15. **"The outfits were quite . . ."** "Meet the Woman Who Inspired Lady Gaga," *Daily News and Analysis*, February 22, 2010, http://www.dnaindia.com/entertainment/report_meet-the-wo man-who-inspired-lady-gaga_1351105.

15. **"Andy's books became . . ."** Grigoriadis, "Growing Up Gaga."

16. **"I have a fascination . . ."** Erika Hobart, "Lady GaGa: Some Like It Pop," *Seattle Weekly*, November 19, 2008, http:// www.seattleweekly.com/2008-11-19/music/lady-ga ga-some-like-it-pop.

17. **She performed for 2.4 million . . .** Lisa Robinson, "In Lady Gaga's Wake," *Vanity Fair*, January 2012, http://www.vanity fair.com/hollywood/2012/01/lady-gaga-201201.

17. **Her popularity skyrocketed . . .** Chris Molanphy, "Introducing the Queen of Pop," *Rolling Stone*, June 29, 2011, http://www .rollingstone.com/music/news/intro ducing-the-queen-of-pop-20110629.

## LESSON 1: FOCUS ON YOUR ONE PERCENTERS

19. **"I'm not the beginning anymore . . ."** Jonathan Van Meter, "Dream Girl," *Vogue*, September 2012.
21. **A 2011 study by Forrester Research . . .** Luca S. Paderni, Corinne Munchbach, and David M. Cooperstein, "The Evolved CMO, 2012," *Forrester Research and Heidrick & Struggles*, February 22, 2012, http://www.heidrick.com/Publications Reports/PublicationsReports/HS_EvolvedCMO2012.pdf.
22. **According to a Satmetrix 2012 Net Promoter Benchmark Study . . .** "Net Promoter U.S. Consumer Benchmarks 2012," Satmetrix, accessed September 24, 2012, http://go.satmetrix .com/rs/satmetrix/images/NPS_Benchmark_Charts_US Consumers_2012-1.pdf.
22. **"Holy sheeit . . ."** Ceee D., review of Time Warner Cable, March 21, 2012, Yelp Austin, http://www.yelp.com/biz/ time-warner-cable-austin#hrid:68gRA9IcYOM7BFcfHt00zg.
23. **"I ate (expletive) . . ."** Christine Spines, "Lady Gaga Wants You," *Cosmopolitan*, April 2009.
24. **This idea of the One Percenters . . .** Ben McConnell and Jackie Huba, *Citizen Marketers: When People Are the Message* (New York: Kaplan Publishing, 2006).
25. **In fact, this was the title . . .** Ben McConnell and Jackie Huba, *Creating Customer Evangelists: How Loyal Customers Become a Volunteer Sales Force*. Rev. ed. (New York: Kaplan Publishing, 2007).
27. **"I don't wanna be one song . . ."** Laura Barton, " 'I've Felt Famous My Whole Life,' " *The Guardian*, January 20, 2009, http://www.guardian.co.uk/music/2009/jan/21/lady-gaga-in terview-fame.
28. **"Why don't we start one . . ."** Neal Pollack, "How Lady Gaga's Manager Reinvented the Celebrity Game with Social Media," *Wired*, June 2012.
29. **"Lady Gaga seems to go . . ."** Ibid.
29. **"Very excited to tell you . . ."** Lady Gaga, Twitter post, August 25, 2012, 11:57 a.m., http://twitter.com/ladygaga.
30. **"They're highly motivated fans . . ."** Pollack, "How Lady Gaga's Manager."
30. **Police in the Indonesian capital city of Jakarta . . .** Bernice Han,

"Lady Gaga Refuses to Tone Down Her Shows: Manager," AFP, May 24, 2012, http://www.google.com/hostednews/afp/article/ALeqM5igciYyUdk7SGRh9pI71Wp-nWSf1A?docId=CNG.d62730d7faba4e00ebc4bff1b1eb1ed4.bf1.

30. **The Islamic Defenders Front (FPI) called Gaga . . .** "Lady Gaga 'Devastated' as Indonesia Concert Cancelled," *BBC News*, May 28, 2012, http://www.bbc.co.uk/news/world-asia-18224783.

31. **"I don't think this has anything . . ."** "Keynote Interview: Troy Carter," YouTube video, 48:51:00, posted by "musicmatterstome," June 20, 2012, http://youtu.be/_qn-OdKCSb0.

31. **In a show of solidarity . . .** James Montgomery, "Lady Gaga's Indonesian Flash Mob Made Her 'Cry So Hard,'" *MTV News*, June 4, 2012, http://www.mtv.com/news/articles/1686476/lady-gaga-indonesia-flash-mob-cry-so-hard.jhtml.

32. **"Tons of rejection . . ."** "Official Indonesian Little Monsters Flash Mob Video," YouTube video, 10:37, posted by "projectlilmonid," June 2, 2012, http://youtu.be/AWqe6EozGro.

32. **"This made me cry . . ."** Lady Gaga, Twitter post, June 4, 2012, 3:10 a.m., http://twitter.com/ladygaga.

32. **It was a moment . . .** Tokiohotelx3r, comment on "Official Indonesian Little Monsters Flash Mob Video," YouTube video, 10:37, posted by "projectlilmonid," accessed September 24, 2012, http://www.youtube.com/all_comments?v=AWqe6EozGro&page=3.

33. **"One of the biggest things . . ."** "Keynote Interview: Troy Carter."

## LESSON 2: LEAD WITH VALUES

35. **"It has nothing to do . . ."** Jonathan Van Meter, "Dream Girl."

37. **"Identity bonds are formed . . ."** Richard Cross and Janet Smith, *Customer Bonding: Pathway to Lasting Customer Loyalty* (Raleigh: NTC/Contemporary Publishing Company, 1996).

38. **Kawasaki shares his experience . . .** Guy Kawasaki, *Selling the Dream* (New York: HarperBusiness, 1992).

39. **"There are artists that . . ."** Corey Sheeran, fan letter to Gaga, Tumblr, accessed September 24, 2012, http://www.tumblr.com/tagged/lady-gaga?before=1343766227.

40. **"The boys picked me up . . ."** Jocelyn Vena, "Lady Gaga Goes Beyond The Fame in Exclusive MTV Special," *MTV News*, May 18, 2011, http://www.mtv.com/news/articles/1664076/lady-gaga-inside-the-outside-special.jhtml.

40. **"Everybody was laughing . . ."** Ibid.

40. **"[For] all the fame and fortune . . ."** Lady Gaga, interview by Oprah Winfrey, *Oprah's Next Chapter*, OWN, March 18, 2012.

41. **"I care only about . . ."** Jeremy Kinser, "Portrait of a Lady," *The Advocate*, July 5, 2011, http://www.advocate.com/arts-entertainment/music/2011/07/05/portrait-lady.

42. **"Dear Mama Monster . . ."** Liza, Minnesota, fan letter to Gaga, accessed September 24, 2012, http://www.tumblr.com/tagged/lady-gaga?before=1343766227.

43. **"The fans lead the music . . ."** Brennan Williams, "Lady Gaga On How Her Fans Inspired Her Social Movement (VIDEO)," *Huffington Post*, December 18, 2011, http://www.huffingtonpost.com/2011/12/14/watch-the-tanning-effect-lady-gaga_n_1146777.html.

44. **"It's about society . . ."** Ibid.

45. **"Together we hope . . ."** Paul Guequierre, "Lady Gaga Ups Her Fight for Nation's Youth, Launches Born This Way Foundation," *HRC Blog* (blog), November 2, 2011, http://www.hrc.org/blog/entry/lady-gaga-ups-her-fight-for-nations-youth-launches-born-this-way-foundation.

45. **Rodemeyer, a passionate Gaga fan . . .** "Jamey Rodemeyer's Suicide Gets Lady Gaga Angry, 'Bullying Is Hate Crime,' " *International Business Times New York*, September 22, 2011, http://newyork.ibtimes.com/articles/218363/20110922/jamey-rodemeyer-lady-gaga-suicide-bully-gay.htm.

45. **"@ladygaga bye mother monster . . ."** Jamey Rodemeyer, Twitter post, September 18, 2011, 12:27 a.m., http://twitter.com/hausofjamey.

45–46. **"The past days . . ."** Lady Gaga, Twitter post, September 21, 2011, 5:00 p.m., http://twitter.com/ladygaga.

46. **Gaga recruited notables . . .** Nicholas D. Kristof, "Born To Not Get Bullied," *The New York Times*, February 29, 2012, http://www.nytimes.com/2012/03/01/opinion/kristof-born-to-not-get-bullied.html.

46. "This is the beginning of a new movement . . ." Lady Gaga, *Oprah's Next Chapter.*

46. "Lady Gaga has used her celebrity . . ." Mark Fidelman, "Meet the Company Behind Lady Gaga's Mega Community that's Turning Brands into Rock Stars," *Forbes*, June 13, 2012, http://www.forbes.com/sites/markfidelman/2012/06/13/meet-the-company-behind-lady-gagas-mega-community-thats-turning-brands-into-rock-stars.

47. "What this is all about . . ." "Harvard Goes Gaga," *Harvard Magazine*, February 29, 2012, http://harvardmagazine.com/2012/02/harvard-goes-gaga.

47. "I'm not here today . . ." Sarah Anne Hughes, "Lady Gaga Launches Born This Way Foundation at Harvard (Video)," *Celebritology* (blog), *Washington Post*, March 1, 2012. http://www.washingtonpost.com/blogs/celebritology/post/lady-gaga-launches-born-this-way-foundation-at-harvard-video/2012/03/01/gIQAUM5LkR_blog.html.

47. "It could be 50 years . . ." Elizabeth S. Auritt, "Lady Gaga Launches the Born This Way Foundation at Harvard," *The Harvard Crimson*, March 1, 2012, http://www.thecrimson.com/article/2012/3/1/lady-gaga-comes-harvard.

47. One such Little Monster . . . "Lady Gaga Sends Toronto School Anti-bullying Video," *CBC News*, November 25, 2011, http://www.cbc.ca/news/canada/toronto/story/2011/11/25/lady-gaga-bullying-school.html.

48. "I got called the gay kid . . ." Ibid.

48. "The subject line said . . ." Ibid.

48. "I just wanted to tell you . . ." Ibid.

49. "I'm starting to actually realize . . ." Ibid.

49. "I love Lady Gaga . . ." Ibid.

50. "You know how you know . . ." Lady Gaga, *Oprah's Next Chapter.*

50–51. A U.S.-based organization called . . . Florida Family Association's Web site, accessed September 24, 2012, http://floridafamily.org/full_article.php?article_no=94.

51. Apparently the FFA was afraid . . . "Lady Gaga's Office Depot Partnership Slammed for Inspiring Teens 'To Embrace Homosexuality,'" *Huffington Post*, July 20, 2012. http://www

.huffingtonpost.com/2012/07/20/lady-gaga-office-depot-part
nership-anti-gay_n_1689809.html.

51. **When a fan thanked Gaga** . . . Lady Gaga, Twitter post, April 1,
2012, 7:55 p.m., http://twitter.com/ladygaga.

51. **She's told fans** . . . "Lady Gaga Talking to Her Fans about
Haters," YouTube video, 0:2:36, posted by "GaGaForeever,"
June 10, 2012, http://youtu.be/f5gsY_XgjMs.

53. **WHAT: Every single company** . . . Simon Sinek, *Start with Why:
How Great Leaders Inspire Everyone to Take Action* (New
York: Portfolio, 2009).

57. **"The counterintuitive fact . . ."** Jack Neff, "How Well-Defined Is
Your Brand's Ideal?" *Advertising Age*, January 16, 2012, http://
adage.com/article/news/defined-brand-s-ideal/232097.

57. **In his book** . . . Jim Stengel, *Grow: How Ideals Power Growth
and Profit at the World's Greatest Companies* (New York:
Crown Business, 2011).

58. **Whole Foods' founder** . . . Danielle Sacks, "John Mackey's
Whole Foods Vision to Reshape Capitalism," *Fast Company*,
December 1, 2009, http://www.fastcompany.com/1460600/
john-mackeys-whole-foods-vision-reshape-capitalism.

58. **From its humble beginnings** . . . "2011 Form 10-K, Whole Foods
Market, Inc." United States Securities and Exchange Commis-
sion, accessed September 29, 2012.

58. **It's ranked No. 264** . . . "Fortune 500," *CNNMoney*, accessed
September 28, 2012, http://money.cnn.com/magazines/fortune/
fortune500/2012/snapshots/10572.html.

59. **"Our Stakeholder Philosophy . . ."** Whole Foods Market 2011
Annual Report, accessed September 29, 2012, http://www
.wholefoodsmarket.com/sites/default/files/media/Global/
Company%20Info/PDFs/ar11.pdf.

59. **"Look, we started when this . . ."** Bonnie Azab Powell, "The
Missionary of Retail: Interview with Whole Foods' Walter
Robb," Bonnie Powell Web site, accessed September 24, 2012,
http://www.bonniepowell.com/wholefoods.html.

60. **"You wrote in a recent article . . ."** Ibid.

60. **Since 2007, Whole Foods** . . . PR Newswire, "Whole Foods
Market Named to 'World's Most Ethical Companies' List," *The
Street*, March 15, 2012, http://www.thestreet.com/

story/11458893/1/whole-foods-mar
ket-named-to-worlds-most-ethical-companies-list.html.

61. "Before I go into detail . . ." Zarfkitty, "Worth the higher prices, in my opinion," Epinions review of Whole Foods, January 3, 2007, http://www.epinions.com/review/Whole_Foods_44829516/content_301198380676?sb=1.

61. According to Method's Facebook page . . . Method's Facebook page, accessed September 24, 2012, http://www.facebook.com/method/info.

62. Lynn Dornblaser, who tracks . . . Mark Borden et al., "The World's Most Innovative Companies," *Fast Company*, March 1, 2008, http://www.fastcompany.com/703052/worlds-most-innovative-companies.

63. Stephen Powers, an analyst . . . Stephanie Clifford and Andrew Martin, "As Consumers Cut Spending, 'Green' Products Lose Allure," *The New York Times*, April 21, 2011, http://www.nytimes.com/2011/04/22/business/energy-environment/22green.html.

63. Powers went on to say . . . Ibid.

64. "It's not that clean products are failing . . ." Ariel Schwartz, "Method: Only Inauthentic 'Green' Cleaning Products Are Failing," *Co.EXIST*, accessed September 24, 2012, http://www.fastcoexist.com/1678022/method-only-inauthentic-green-cleaning-products-are-failing.

64. He acknowledges that the big brands . . . Ibid.

64. In her blog *Stain Removal 101* . . . Taylor, "Method All Purpose Cleaner Reviews and Uses," *Stain-Removal-101*, accessed September 24, 2012, http://www.stain-removal-101.com/method-all-purpose-cleaner.html.

65. "The ideal—the higher-order benefit . . ." Stengel, *Grow: How Ideals Power Growth*.

65. And as Eric Ryan tells Stengel . . . Ibid.


**LESSON 3: BUILD COMMUNITY**

67. "The instrument that I never learned . . ." Lady Gaga, interview by Robin Roberts and George Stephanopoulos, *Good Morning America*, ABC News, May 27, 2011, http://abcnews.go.com/

GMA/video/lady-gaga-interview-gma-con cert-dream-true-13701895.

69. **"Ever since that first time . . ."** Anja, fan letter to Gaga, Tumblr, accessed September 25, 2012, http://www.tumblr.com/tagged/ dear-mama-monter?before=1330372161.

71. **"The turning point for me . . ."** Jocelyn Vena, "Lady Gaga On Success: 'The Turning Point for Me Was the Gay Community,' " *MTV News*, May 7, 2009, http://www.mtv.com/news/articles/ 1610781/lady-gaga-on-success-turn ing-point-me-was-gay-community.jhtml.

71. **"My love for my gay fans . . ."** Jeremy Kinser, "Portrait of a Lady."

72. **"I was called really horrible . . ."** Kristof, "Born To Not Get Bullied."

72. **"It's funny because some friends . . ."** Vena, "Lady Gaga On Success."

73. **She laments about her . . .** Mother Monster [Lady Gaga], "A letter to my sweet fans," *Littlemonsters.com*, accessed September 25, 2012, http://littlemonsters.com/text/ 502a26e8ac460c3c27001ebc.

74. **"I start to think about all of the people . . ."** "Lady Gaga Presents: The Monster Ball Tour at Madison Square Garden," filmed November 21, 2011, HBO Concert Event, Streamline/ Kon Live/Interscope, directed by Laurieann Gibson.

75. **"She's done a masterful job . . ."** Erin Nelson, interview by Jackie Huba, July 16, 2012.

75. **"She's done a tremendous job . . ."** Ibid.

76. **"The Monster Ball is in essence . . ."** Lady Gaga, interview by Larry King, *Larry King Live*, CNN, June 1, 2010, http:// transcripts.cnn.com/TRANSCRIPTS/1006/01/lkl.01.html.

76. **"The Monster Ball will set you free! . . ."** "The Monster Ball— Dialogue Transcript," *Gagapedia*, accessed September 25, 2012, http://ladygaga.wikia.com/wiki/The_Monster_Ball_-_ Dialogue_transcript.

77. **"What I do is, in essence . . ."** James Dinh, "Lady Gaga Wants Fans to 'Feel Alive' During Monster Ball Show," *MTV News*, December 28, 2009, http://www.mtv.com/news/articles/ 1628763/lady-gaga-wants-fans-feel-alive-during-mon ster-ball-show.jhtml.

77. **The first thing you see . . .** Welcome screen, Littlemonsters .com, accessed September 29, 2012, http://Littlemonsters.com.

77. **Fans are encouraged . . .** Ibid.

77. **Because Gaga's fans . . .** "Little Monsters Chat, Scaling and Future Features . . ." *Backplane* (blog), August 6, 2012, http://thebackplane.tumblr.com/post/28881441021/little-monsters-chat-scaling-and-future-features.

78. **"We reached 1 Billion views on youtube . . ."** Lady Gaga, Twitter post, October 24, 2010, 7:35, a.m., http://twitter.com/ladygaga.

78. **"I'm humbled + honored . . ."** Lady Gaga, Twitter post, December 1, 2011, 1:45 a.m., http://twitter.com/ladygaga.

78. **"#PawsUp for our album's being nominated . . ."** Lady Gaga, Twitter post, December 1, 2011, 1:49 a.m., http://twitter.com/ladygaga.

78. **On August 25, 2012, she tweeted . . .** Lady Gaga, Twitter post, August 25, 2012, 11:57 a.m., http://twitter.com/ladygaga.

79. **The premise of the film . . .** "Google Chrome: Lady Gaga," YouTube video, 1:31, posted by "googlechrome," May 20, 2011, http://youtu.be/sDPJ-o1leAw.

79. **Gaga's team collected . . .** Tim Nudd, "Google Mashes Up Fan Videos for Lady Gaga Spot," *Adweek*, May 23, 2001, http://www.adweek.com/adfreak/google-mashes-fan-videos-lady-gaga-spot-131913.

80. **Yezak spliced together . . .** "Happy Birthday Lady Gaga Biggest Fan Made Video Ever," YouTube video, 9:47, posted by "RyanJamesYezak," March 25, 2010, http://youtu.be/3Q7CKmeaOuM.

80. **"I've never cried so hard . . ."** Lady Gaga, Twitter post, March 28, 2010, 6:54 p.m., http://twitter.com/ladygaga.

80. **Fans posted letters online . . .** "Dear Mama Monster," Tumblr site, accessed September 25, 2012, http://dear-mama-monster .tumblr.com.

81. **The girls posted the eight-minute video . . .** "Dear Mother Monster: A Thank You from All Your Fans," YouTube video, 7:59, posted by "GCMsPiCeS," July 30, 2012, http://youtu.be/lT689rlZ4Uc.

81. **"Can't breathe . . ."** "Dear Mama Monster Project," comment on *Littlemonsters.com*, accessed September 24, 2012, http://littlemonsters.com/video/5017b95dc84b0aff77001de6.

81. **"Your little monsters love you . . ."** Ibid.
82. **Fiskars' own brand research . . .** "Fiskateers," Brains on Fire Web site, accessed September 28, 2012, http://www.brainson fire.com/work/view/fiskateers.
82. **Brains on Fire set up 150 interviews . . .** B. L. Ochman, "Fiskateers Case Study: How a Social Community Became a Veritable Sales Force," *What's Next Blog*, October 15, 2008, http://www.whatsnextblog.com/2008/10/fiskateers_how_a_social_community_became_a_veritable_sales_force.
83. **Fiskars (with the help of Brains on Fire) . . .** "Fisk-a-History 101," *Fiskateers* (blog), accessed September 25, 2012, http://fiskateers.com/blog/fiskateer-history.
83. **What the road trip showed . . .** Ibid.
84. **For example, during the first year . . .** Robbin Phillips et al., *Brains on Fire: Igniting Powerful, Sustainable Word of Mouth Movements* (Hoboken, NJ: Wiley, 2010).
84. **"There's a genuine love . . ."** "Why I Love Being a Fiskateer," YouTube video, 1:56, posted by "AFiskateer," April 15, 2009, http://youtu.be/MQKOHeTn69c.
87. **"In the MINI community it's all about belonging or showing off . . ."** Ray Schiel, " 'Do You Hear What I Hear?': Listening to the Community, an Interview with MotiveQuest's Tom O'Brien," December 2, 2008, http://www.globalsocialmedia network.com/?tag=mini-cooper.
88. **It's a kind of tribal . . .** Ibid.
88. **In 2012, approximately six thousand people . . .** Jason Udy, "Mini Takes the States from New York to Los Angeles," *Motor Trend*, July 21, 2012, http://wot.motortrend.com/mini-takes-the-states-from-new-york-to-los-angeles-235085.html.
88. **Its June 2012 sales were up 14.7 percent . . .** Scott Burgess, "Mini Takes the States: Brits Re-invade Washington on 200th Anniversary of War of 1812," *Autoblog* (blog), July 5, 2012, http://www.autoblog.com/2012/07/05/mini-takes-the-states-brits-re-invade-washing ton-on-200th-anniv.
88. **It also won the Polk Automobile Loyalty Award . . .** "MINI Honored With Polk Automotive Loyalty Award: MINI Cooper Awarded Top Spot in the Compact Car Category," BMW

Group Press Release, January 14, 2010, http://press.bmwgroup
.com/shTXF.

## LESSON 4: GIVE FANS A NAME

91. "We identify with each other . . ." Lady Gaga, interview by
Touré, "Lady Gaga: On the Record with Fuse," *Fuse*, December 7, 2009.

93. "I wrote the album . . ." Lady Gaga, interview by Larry King.

95. While at the show, Gaga . . . Twitter post, February 1, 2010,
11:06 a.m., http://twitter.com/ladygaga.

95. "The hands were based . . ." Mi2N, "Lady Gaga, Elton John
and a Beautiful Baldwin," *Music Dish*, February 12, 2010,
http://www.musicdish.com/mag/index.php3?id=12591.

95. Hours after the show . . . Lady Gaga, Twitter post, February 1,
2010, 2:08 a.m., http://twitter.com/ladygaga.

95. Her tweet explained . . . Lady Gaga, Twitter post, February 2,
2010, 4:39 p.m., http://twitter.com/ladygaga.

96. *Forbes* writer Judy Martin likened Gaga . . . Judy Martin, "Lady
Gaga and the Power of the Feminine Brand," *Forbes*, May 19,
2011, http://www.forbes.com/sites/work-in-prog
ress/2011/05/19/lady-gaga-power-feminine-brand.

97. "Maker's [had] started . . ." Bill Samuels Jr., interview by Ben
McConnell and Jackie Huba, *Church of the Customer Podcast*,
January 10, 2006, http://www.creatingcustomerevangelists
.com/podcasts/churchofthecustomer-01-10-06.mp3.

98. " 'I got an idea that . . .' " Ibid.

100. "We never worry about the fact . . ." Ibid.

102. "Dayle Hall, Aruba Networks senior director . . ." Dayle Hall,
interview by Jackie Huba, October 2, 2012.

102. they have access to a wide variety of professional development
opportunities . . . "Aruba Networks Launches Airheads
Community for Enterprise Mobility Experts," *MediaBuzz*,
March 2012, http://www.mediabuzz.com.sg/archives/2012/
march/1517-aruba-networks-launches-airheads-commu
nity-for-enterprise-mobility-experts.

103. "Within the Airheads community, I can share my experience . . ." "Aruba Networks Launches Airheads Community for

Enterprise Mobility Experts," Aruba Networks News Releases, December 5, 2011, http://www.arubanetworks.com/ news-releases/aruba-networks-launches-airheads-commu nity-for-enterprise-mobility-experts.

### LESSON 5: EMBRACE SHARED SYMBOLS

105. "I . . . try to create things . . ." Lady Gaga, interview by Larry King.

109. "It was a very exciting moment . . ." "Lady Gaga Monster Ball Tour-Monster Claw and Audience Call," YouTube video, 4:20, posted by "iBEdebbie115," December 24, 2009, http://youtu .be/1bBhTrlBKRA.

110. She told the *Big Top 40 Show* . . . Lewis Corner, "GaGa Inspired by My Little Pony," *Digital Spy*, March 7, 2011, http:// www.digitalspy.co.uk/music/news/a307561/gaga-in spired-by-my-little-pony.html.

111. "Highway Unicorn is about me . . ." Lady Gaga, Twitter post, May 22, 2011, 8:12 p.m., http://twitter.com/ladygaga.

112. Lady Gaga's stylist, Nicola Formichetti . . . Lee Carter, "The Incredible But True Story of How Nicola Formichetti Got Rick Genest to Model in Mugler," *Hint Fashion Magazine*, March 20, 2011, http://www.hintmag.com/post/the-true-story-of-how-nico la-formichetti-got-rick-genest-the-guy-with-a-scalp-tat too-to-model-in-mugler-march-20-2011.

114. "I am not a gimmick guy . . ." Myron Cope, *Myron Cope: Double Yoi!* (Champaign, IL: Sports Publishing, 2002).

114. "I'm a gimmick guy . . ." Ibid.

114. Brainstorming with his boss, Cope said the gimmick . . . Ibid.

115. "We'll call it the Terrible Towel . . ." Greg Garber, " 'Terrible' Influence Yields Good Results," *ESPN*, January 29, 2009, http://sports.espn.go.com/nfl/playoffs2008/columns/ story?columnist=garber_greg&page=hotread20/garber.

115. "The Terrible Towel is poised to strike . . ." Ibid.

116. "All of a sudden . . ." Ibid.

116. "Nearing kickoff, the Steelers gathered . . ." Myron Cope, *Myron Cope.*

116. "I think every great nation . . ." Greg Garber, " 'Terrible' Influence."

117. "We thought they wanted . . ." Chuck Salter, "How the Lance Armstrong Foundation Became Livestrong," *Fast Company*, October 26, 2010, http://www.fastcompany.com/1698037/ how-lance-armstrong-foundation-became-livestrong.

117. "HE LOVED IT . . ." Ibid.

118. According to Kat Jones . . . Ibid.

118. "When I heard that Nike . . ." Sal Ruibal, "Livestrong Bracelets Approaching 50 Million Strong," *USA Today*, May 12, 2005, http://www.usatoday.com/sports/cycling/2005-05-12-live strong_x.htm.

118. According to Livestrong executives . . . Brent Schrotenboer, "Livestrong: Only 8 Donors Asked For Their Money Back," *USA Today*, November 12, 2012, http://www.usatoday.com/ story/sports/cycling/2012/11/12/livestrong-lance-armstrong-doping/1700831/.

119. Livestrong is the rare example . . . Chuck Salter, "How the Lance Armstrong."

### LESSON 6: MAKE THEM FEEL LIKE ROCK STARS

121. "Dear Mama Monster . . ." Erika, fan letter to Gaga, Tumblr, accessed September 25, 2012, http://dear-mama-monster .tumblr.com/post/28497360065/dear-mama-mon ster-my-name-is-erika-you-pulled-my.

124. "I hope they're not busy . . ." "Lady Gaga Monster Ball Tour—Monster Claw and Audience Call."

125. "I'm sending up some people . . ." Ibid.

125. This partnership was part . . . Rebecca Sebek, "Lady Gaga: Singer, Fashion Artist and Philanthropist," *Halogen,* accessed September 25, 2012, http://halogentv.com/articles/ lady-gaga-singer-fashion-artist-and-philanthropist.

126. "This is a necklace . . ." Lady Gaga, Twitter post, April 27, 2012, 2:10 a.m., http://twitter.com/ladygaga.

126. "The real monster pit key . . ." Lady Gaga, Twitter post, April 27, 2012, 2:16 a.m., http://twitter.com/ladygaga.

126. Gaga has been posting pictures . . . Mother Monster [Lady Gaga], "HOLDER OF THE KEY TO THE MONSTER PIT IN PARIS 9.22.2012: MAUD MECHURA," Littlemonsters.com,

accessed September 25, 2012, http://littlemonsters.com/
image/5061d8554f5cf1d477001220.

128. **"When I was your age . . ."** "Lady Gaga Brings Fan Larissa
On Stage—Vienna 2012," YouTube video, 3:17, posted by
"paxovismc44," August 20, 2012, http://youtu
.be/7SIXDFUFxyA.

128. **"Then one day . . ."** Ibid.

128. **"It could be you . . ."** Ibid.

129. **"There's no dream . . ."** Ibid.

129. **At the Brisbane, Australia, stop . . .** "Lady Gaga—Bad Kids—
Live in Stockholm, Sweden 31.08.2012 HD," YouTube video,
4:30, posted by "LauiiiHD," September 1, 2012, http://youtu
.be/wcnaIyeTc2c.

130. **One particular drawing . . .** Helen Green, "Disney Gaga!"
*Littlemonsters.com*, accessed September 25, 2012, http://
littlemonsters.com/image/4fd8d59aec64fee47e0000e3.

131. **"This is my favorite thing . . ."** Lady Gaga, Twitter post, July
25, 2012, 2:32 p.m., http://twitter.com/ladygaga.

131. **"LADIES, GENTLEMEN, MONSTERS, AND PRINCESS
HIGHs,"** Littlemonsters.com, accessed September 25, 2012,
http://littlemonsters.com/text/504e9286b2d03c913
d001354.

131. **"This is so incredible . . ."** Helen Green, comment on "LA-
DIES, GENTLEMEN, MONSTERS, AND PRINCESS
HIGHs," *Littlemonsters.com*, accessed September 25, 2012,
http://,/text/504e9286b2d03c913d001354.

133. **"Then, complete strangers . . ."** Rod Brooks, "Celebrity like
greeting as I arrived in Austin (Photos no doubt to come)!"
Facebook post, April 20, 2010, https://www.facebook.com/
notes/rod-brooks/celebrity-like-greeting-as-i-arrived-in-au
stin-photos-no-doubt-to-come/424193310147.

135. **"The outcome was spectacular . . ."** Sean McDonald, "WOM
Lesson: Celebrate Customers," *Ant's Eye View* (blog), May 24,
2010, http://www.antseyeview.com/blog/wom-lesson-cele
brate-customers.

135. **"The seed of the concept . . ."** Spike Jones, e-mail message to
Jackie Huba, August 19, 2012.

136. **"We didn't give him a script . . ."** Ibid.

137. "It was an event . . ." Daphne, "eBay Live! 2002 . . . A Look Back," *The Chatter: eBay Community Newsletter* 2, no. 5 (March 2003), http://pages.ebay.com/community/chatter/2003Mar/eblive.html.

137. "Most companies are defined . . ." Ibid.

138. Customers were "blown away" . . . texas-auctions, "THANKS EBAY for the Red Carpet Applause," *eBay Live! Community Conference* discussion board, June 17, 2006, http://forums.ebay.com/db1/topic/Ebay-Live-Community/Thanks-Ebay-For/1000303415&.

138. "This was one of those great . . ." "Highlights from the 2008 Ebay Live Gala at Chicago's McCormick Place," YouTube video, 7:05, posted by "scottyluvslucy," July 18, 2008, http://youtu.be/tQJYLRAf7_c.

138. As a side note, eBay Live! was discontinued . . . "EBay Live! Now Dead," Reuters, July 14, 2009, http://www.reuters.com/article/2009/07/14/us-ebay-idUSTRE56D5SH20090714?feedType=RSS&feedName=technologyNews.

138. They have been partnering . . . Brad and Debra Schepp, "Behind the Scenes at eBay: On Location; Dallas Seller Extravaganza Was a Red Carpet Affair," *Auctiva*, May 24, 2010, http://www.auctiva.com/edu/entry.aspx?id=Behind-the-Scenes-at-eBay-On-Location.

**LESSON 7: GENERATE SOMETHING TO TALK ABOUT**

141. "When you make music . . ." Elizabeth Goodman, "Collect Call from . . . Lady Gaga," *Blender*, April 2009.

143. You have to create a "purple cow," . . . Seth Godin, *Purple Cow: Transform Your Business by Being Remarkable* (New York: Portfolio, 2003).

144. "I'm a true academic . . ." "Lady Gaga on 'Mastering the Art of Fame,'" *CBS News*, February 14, 2011, http://www.cbsnews.com/2102-18560_162-7337078.html.

144. "You know, I feel so so happy . . ." BestStatus, September 5, 2012 (2:50 p.m.), comment on "Lady Gaga Debuts an 'ART-POP' Invention," *GagaDaily*, http://gagadaily.com/index.php?showtopic=29384&st=120#entry1681086.

145. **"I never thought I'd be asking Cher . . ."** Caryn Ganz, "Meet the Mystery Meat Dress: Lady Gaga Explains Rare VMAs Outfit," *Yahoo Music*, September 12, 2010, http://music.yahoo.com/blogs/stop-the-presses/meet-the-mystery-meat-dress-lady-gaga-explains-rare-vmas-outfit.html.

145. **PETA denounced the dress . . .** Laura Roberts, "Lady Gaga's Meat Dress Divides Opinion," *The Telegraph*, September 14, 2010, http://www.telegraph.co.uk/culture/music/music-news/8001267/Lady-Gagas-meat-dress-divides-opinion.html.

145–46. **Vegetarian singer Morrissey . . .** Michael Deacon, "Morrissey On . . . Lady Gaga and Modern Pop," *The Telegraph*, June 17, 2011, http://www.telegraph.co.uk/culture/music/8579607/Morrissey-on . . . -Lady-Gaga-and-modern-pop.html.

146. *Time* **magazine went on to name . . .** Belinda Luscombe, "The Top 10 Fashion Statements," *Time*, December 9, 2010, http://www.time.com/time/specials/packages/article/0,28804,2035319_2034464_2034435,00.html.

146. **"Meat purse was genius! . . ."** Cher, Twitter post, September 13, 2010, 11:03 a.m., http://twitter.com/cher.

146. **She had previously spoken out . . .** Dan Zak, "Lady Gaga, Already a Gay Icon, Shows She's an Activist Too," *Washington Post*, October 12, 2009, http://www.washingtonpost.com/wp-dyn/content/article/2009/10/11/AR2009101101892.html?sid=ST2009101101924.

146. **"These soldiers that are . . ."** Jocelyn Vena, "Lady Gaga's Best Awards-Show Arrivals: From Kermit to the Egg," *MTV News*, February 14, 2011, http://www.mtv.com/news/articles/1657931/lady-gaga-egg-arrival-grammys.jhtml.

147. **Gaga paid for the veterans . . .** Gil Kaufman, "Lady Gaga's White-Carpet Guests Talk VMA VIP Experience," *MTV News*, September 13, 2010, http://www.mtv.com/news/articles/1647759/lady-gagas-white-carpet-guests-talk-vma-vip-experience.jhtml.

147. **"It is a devastation to me . . ."** Ganz, "Meet the Mystery Meat Dress."

147. **"If we don't stand up . . ."** Ibid.

147. **"Gay Veterans were my VMA dates . . ."** Lady Gaga, Twitter post, September 14, 2010, 8:48 a.m., http://twitter.com/ladygaga.

147. **Reid tweeted back . . .** Senator Harry Reid, Twitter post, September 14, 2010, 11:19 a.m., http://twitter.com/HarryReid.

148. **"If you dig a little deeper . . ."** Brett Zongker, "Lady Gaga's Meat Dress to Be Shown in DC Museum," Associated Press, September 6, 2012.

149. **"I raised an eyebrow . . ."** Jonathan Van Meter, "Dream Girl."

149. **"It must smell enticing . . ."** Ibid.

149 **"I was pregnant at that time . . ."** Ibid.

149. **"She was really behind . . ."** Ibid.

150. **"We [myself and photographer Steven Klein] thought . . ."** Ibid.

150. **With six million bottles selling . . .** Lady Gaga, Twitter post, September 22, 2011, 6:18 a.m., http://twitter.com/ladygaga.

150. **"She is an artist . . ."** "Gaga's 'Blood and Semen' Perfume Outsells Beyonce and Madonna," *ANI*, September 1, 2012, http://zeenews.india.com/entertainment/glamtalk/gaga-s-blood-and-semen-perfume-outsells-beyonce-and-madonna_118273.htm.

151. **"Lady Gaga is incubating . . ."** Sheila Marikar and Eileen Murphy, "Lady Gaga Arrives at Grammys in Giant Egg," *ABC News*, February 13, 2011, http://abcnews.go.com/Entertainment/lady-gaga-arrives-grammys-giant-egg/story?id=12908509#.UGJp3EIZe-J.

151. **"You will not believe your eyes . . ."** Kelly Osbourne, Twitter post, February 13, 2011, 3:51 p.m., http://twitter.com/MissKellyO.

152. **As Gaga later explained on *The Tonight Show* . . .** "Lady Gaga Visits Jay Leno," Dailymotion video, 12:45, posted by "Erhan Dalfidan," Feburary 15, 2011, http://www.dailymotion.com/video/xh1hh1_lady-gaga-visits-jay-leno_music.

152. ***Billboard* later said that in the fifty-two years of music . . .** Bill Werde, "Lady Gaga 'Born This Way' Cover Story," *Billboard*, February 18, 2011, http://www.billboard.com/news/lady-gaga-born-this-way-cover-story-1005041172.story.

152. **Elton John said the song . . .** Tanner Stransky, "Lady Gaga and Elton John: Working Together on the Pop Queen's New Album," *EW.com*, October 7, 2010, 5:37 pm, http://music-mix.ew.com/2010/10/07/lady-gaga-elton-john-new-album.

153. "I wanted to put my money exactly . . ." Werde, "Lady Gaga 'Born This Way' Cover Story."

154. "I was thinking about birth . . ." "Lady Gaga Visits Jay Leno."

154. "Not only did we take home some awards . . ." "Lady Gaga Dishes On Grammy Vessel & On Stage Birth," *Access Hollywood*, February 17, 2011, http://www.accesshollywood.com/ lady-gaga-reveals-inspiration-behind-born-this-way-gram my-performance_article_44050.

155. She announced to fans on Littlemonsters.com . . . Mother Monster [Lady Gaga], "ARTPOP is not just an ALBUM its a PROJECT," *Littlemonsters.com,* accessed September 30, 2012, http://littlemonsters.com/text/5047d491ac460c3508001b8e.

155. "You inspired me to create something . . ." Ibid.

155. Gaga has had "mind-blowing, irresponsible, condomless sex" . . . Goodman, "Collect Call from . . . Lady Gaga."

156. "We first got our needles out nine years ago . . ." "The Big Knit," Innocent, accessed September 25, 2012, http://www .innocentdrinks.co.uk/bigknit.

156. In 2011, 1.5 million hats were sent . . . Lara O'Reilly, "Q&A with Innocent Marketing Director Douglas Lamont," *Marketing Week,* September 6, 2012, http://www.marketingweek .co.uk/news/qa-with-innocent-marketing-director-doug las-lamont/4003670.article.

158. The company explains on the RoadBurn blog . . . "RoadBurn 2008: The Chronicles of Three Freshbookers Across the Southern United States," *FreshBooks* (blog), accessed September 25, 2012, http://roadburn.freshbooks.com.

158. "[Our three-person team] had eleven meals . . ." Becky Carroll, "FreshBooks Rocks: Getting Personal with Customers," *Customers Rock!* (blog), April 2, 2008, http://customersrock .wordpress.com/2008/04/02/freshbooks-rocks-getting-per sonal-with-customers.

159. He says, "The buzz came from the fact that we met . . ." "Five Questions for FreshBooks," *One Degree*, April 15, 2008, http://www.onedegree.ca/2008/04/five-questions.html.

159. "Our goals for the trip . . ." Ibid.

160. According to Saul, they "were able to track . . ." Ibid.

160. "Customers are always more than . . ." Ibid.

160. "It's clearly too bad . . ." Donna Vitan, April 2nd, 2008 (11:28 p.m.) comment on Saul Colt, "Our Trip May Be Over but the Adventure Isn't!" *FreshBooks* (blog), March 8, 2008, http://roadburn.freshbooks.com/2008/03/18/our-trip-may-be-over-but-the-adventure-isnt.

160. "I was shocked when you came through Boston . . ." Joseph Crawford, September 8, 2011 (10:30 a.m.) comment on Saul Colt, "FreshBooks Is Going 'On the Road Again,' " *FreshBooks* (blog), September 3, 2011, http://www.freshbooks.com/blog/2011/09/03/freshbooks-is-going-on-the-road-again.

**BUILDING MONSTER LOYALTY OF YOUR OWN**

163. "I believe that everyone . . ." Grigoriadis, "Growing Up Gaga."

# SELECTED RESOURCES

## LADY GAGA'S SOCIAL SITES

Twitter.com/ladygaga
Facebook.com/ladygaga
Plus.google.com/+LadyGaga/
YouTube.com/ladygagaofficial
YouTube.com/LadyGagaVEVO
Littlemonsters.com

## OTHER SOURCES

Bornthiswayfoundation.org
GagaDaily.com
GagaNews.com
PropaGaga.com

# INDEX

*Advocate, The,* 41
Age UK, 156
Akon, 16–17
Anja (Gaga fan), 69–70
Anti-Doping Agency, U.S., 118
Ant's Eye View, 132–35, *134*
Apple, 38, 42, 54, *54*
Arm & Hammer Essentials, 64
Armstrong, Lance, 117, 118, 119
*ARTPOP,* 155
Aruba Airheads, 97, 101–3
Aruba Networks, 101–3
Associated Press, 148

Backplane, 28
"Bad Romance," 17, 109, 145, 154
Bain & Company, 174
Baltimore Colts, 115, 116
Bazaarvoice, 5, 75
BBC Radio, 5
Beatles, 39
"Best Status" (GagaDaily user),
    144–45
Big Knit, 156–57, *157*
*Big Top 40 Show,* 110
*Billboard,* 3, 17, 152

BMW, 88
*Born this Way,* 5, 41, 78, 111
"Born this Way," 6, 41, 49, 109–
    10, 111–12, 152, 153, 168
    message of, 50
Born This Way Ball Tour, 30, 51,
    75, 81, *110*, 111, 121, 126, *127*,
    128, 129, 131
Born This Way Foundation, 45–47,
    51, 168
Bowie, David, 16
Brains on Fire, 82, 83
branding, 107, 123
Bree (Gaga fan), 1
Brooks, Rod, 133–35, *134*
bullying, 40, 43, 45–46, 48–49, 51,
    72, 96, 152, 168

California Endowment, 45
Calloway, Sway, 146
Canadian Broadcasting Company,
    48
Carroll, Becky, 158
Carter, Troy, 27, 28, 29–31, 73,
    75
Celeb 4 a Day, 133

Certified Fiskars Demonstrators (CFDs), 84
Chanel No. 5, 150
Cher, 145, 146
Chevrolet, 135–37
Chevy Ignites, 135–36
Chopra, Deepak, 46
*Church of the Customer,* 5
*Citizen Marketers* (Huba & McConnell), 24
Clorox Green Works, 63, 64
Coca-Cola, 5
Collaborative Arts Project 21, 12
collective experiences, 75–77, 84
Colt, Saul, 158–60
community building, 69–89, 169–71
Cooper, Anderson, 144
Cope, Myron, 114–16
*Cosmopolitan,* 23
Cotton, Tom, 137
Coty Beauty, 149–50
Cox, Courtney, 128
Crawford, Joseph, 160
*Creating Customer Evangelists* (Huba), 25
Cross, Richard, 37
Crow, Sheryl, 118
*Customer Bonding: Pathway to Lasting Customer Loyalty* (Cross & Smith), 37
customer loyalty, 3–5, 6, 13, 18, 21–23, 37–38
customer satisfaction, 22–23

Dallas Cowboys, 116
"Dancing in the Dark," 128
Darling, Darian, 15
"Dear Mother Monster Project," 80–81
DeGeneres, Ellen, 147

Disney, 130–31
"Don't Ask, Don't Tell" (DADT) policy, 71, 146–47, 168
Dornblaser, Lynn, 62

eBay, 137–38
eBay Live!, 137, 138
"Edge of Glory, The," 79
Epinions.com, 61
equality issues, 71
Erika (Gaga fan), 121
ESPN, 114
Ethisphere Institute's World's Most Ethical Companies, 60–61
Etobicoke School of the Arts, 47

Facebook, 4, 27, 28, 29, 30, 62, 112, 123, 130, 133, 157
Factory, 108
*Fame, The,* 4, 17, 93, 95
Fame (Gaga's perfume), 149–50
Fame Ball Tour, 75
*Fame Monster, The,* 17, 93
*Fast Company,* 117
Fergie, 15
Fiskafriendzy, 84
Fiskars, 81, 82–85, 86, 87, 169
Five Dimensions of a Cause, 38–52
Fleishman-Hillard, 135–36
Florida Family Association (FFA), 50, 51
*Forbes,* 3, 96
Formichetti, Nicola, 112
Forrester Research, 21
Fortune 500, 58
Fortune 1000, 132
FreshBooks, 158–60
FreshBooks RoadBurn, 156, 158–59
Fusari, Rob, 14
Future of Web Apps, 159

Gaff, Jared, 136–37
GagaDaily.com, 27, 145
GagaNews.com, 28
Gaynor, Gloria, 152
gay rights, 146–48
Genest, Rick, 112
Germanotta, Cynthia, 12, 45
Germanotta, Joe, 12, 14
Germanotta, Stefani Joanne Ange-
    lina, see Lady Gaga
Godin, Seth, 143
Golden Circle, 52–55, 52
Google, 112
Google Chrome, 79
Grammy Awards, 3, 41, 78, 94–95,
    151, 151, 153, 154
Green, Helen, 130–32
Grow: How Ideals Power Growth
    and Profit at the World's Great-
    est Companies (Stengel), 57,
    64–65
Guardian, The, 27

Hall, Dayle, 102
Harvard University, 45, 46
Haus of Gaga, 6, 108, 131
HBO, 74
Heidrick & Struggles, 21
"Highway Unicorn," 111
Hilton, Perez, 5
homelessness, 112, 125
homosexuality, 45–46, 48, 50, 71,
    112, 125, 146–48, 152, 168
House of Mugler, 153
Huffington Post, 44
Hussein Chalayan, 153

IBM, 38
Indonesia, 30–31, 50
Innocent, 156–57, 157
International Space Station, 116

Islamic Defenders Front (FPI), 30
It Gets Better Project, 45
It's Not About the Bike: My Jour-
    ney Back to Life (Armstrong),
    117
"I Will Survive," 152

Jackson, Michael, 39
Jennings, Zach, 103
Jobs, Steve, 54
John, Elton, 94, 94, 152
Jones, Katherine, 117, 118, 119
Jones, Spike, 135
"Just Dance," 16, 17

Kawasaki, Guy, 38
Kerry, John, 118
King, Larry, 76, 93
Kinney, Taylor, 73
Klein, Steven, 150
Koh, Terence, 94–95, 94
Kon Live, 16–17
"Konvicted," 16
Kristof, Nicholas, 72

Lady Gaga, 3, 94, 151
    as authentic, 73–75
    awards won by, 3
    big effects generated by, 44–47,
        147
    bonding with fans by, 4, 5,
        44–45
    childhood bullying of, 40, 43
    community building by, 69–82,
        89, 169–70
    fan collaboration and, 79–82,
        155
    fan loyalty of, 3–7, 11, 13, 17–18,
        23, 30–32, 69, 123, 167, 176
    fans as rockstars and, 123–27,
        173–74

Lady Gaga (*cont.*)
    fan sites for, 27–29
    fans recruited by, 30
    fortune made by, 3
    gay community supported by,
        71, 112, 125, 146–48, 168,
        169
    Golden Circle of, 55
    as innovative, 144, 149
    international fan base of, 31–32
    investment in fan base by, 27, 29
    as misunderstood, 23
    Monster Pit Key and, 126–27
    as music prodigy, 12–13
    origin of stage name, 14
    people polarized by, 49–52
    perfume made by, 148–50
    persona of, 14, 27
    Phone a Monster and, 124–25
    piano played by, 12–13
    positive influence on fans of, 6,
        42–44
    quotes from, 9, 19, 35, 67, 91,
        105, 141, 163
    selfless actions of, 47–49
    shared symbols and, 107–13,
        172
    social media used by, 5, 28–30,
        78, 130–32
    song writing by, 15
    spotlight gifts and, 129–30
    standing out and, 143–56,
        174–75
    as subject of protests, 30–31,
        50–51
    tattoos of, 95, 111
    the vessel and, 151–56, 151
    vision embodied by, 39–42, 65
    wild performances and outfits of,
        4, 7, 12, 15, 16, 30–31, 76,
        108, 144, 145–48, 153

LadyGagaNow.net, 27
*Lady Gaga Presents: The Monster
    Ball Tour at Madison Square
    Garden,* 74
Lauper, Cyndi, 71
Leno, Jay, 152, 154
"Let's Dance," 27
Littlemonsters.com, 28–30, 43, 73,
    77, 78, 80, 96, 126, 127, 130,
    144, 155
Livestrong bracelets, 113, 117–19
Livestrong Foundation, 117, 119
Liza (Gaga fan), 43
Los Angeles Nokia Center, 147
"Love Game," 17
Lowry, Adam, 62, 65
loyalty programs, 98
Lyne, Laura, 28–29

MacArthur Foundation, 45
McConnell, Ben, 24, 97
MAC Cosmetics, 71
McDerment, Mike, 158
McDonald, Sean, 133, 135
Mackey, John, 58
McQueen, Alexander, 146
Maker's Mark Ambassadors, 97–
    101, 99, 102, 170
marketing:
    branding and, 107
    community building and, 69–89,
        169–71
    customer loyalty and, 3–5, 11,
        21–23
    customers as peers and, 70
    customer satisfaction and, 22–23
    five dimensions of a cause and,
        38–52
    Golden Circle and, 52–66
    identity bonds and, 37, 44, 52
    investing in customer base and, 27

making customers rockstars and, 123–39, 173–74

One Percenters and, 24–27, 29–30, 32–33, 93–104, 143, 165–76

shared symbols and, 107–20, 172–73

Shiny New Object syndrome and, 21, 22

stakeholder philosophy and, 59, 60

standing out and, 143–61, 174–75

values and, 37–38, 39, 42, 57, 58–59, 61–62, 168–69

"Marry the Night," 128, 129

Martin, Colleen (Lady Starlight), 14–15

Martin, Judy, 96

meat dress, 145–48

Meetup.com, 86

Mercury, Freddie, 14

Method, 61–65

Michaels, 84

Milkshake Media, 117

Millward Brown Optimor, 56, 57

Minaj, Nicki, 27

MINI, 81, 86–89

MINI Cooper, 86

MINI Meetup group, 86

MINI Takes the States, 88

MINIUSA.com, 87

Mintel, 62

Mobile Virtual Enterprise (MOVE), 101

Monster Ball Tour, 17, 75, 76–77, 109, 124–25

monster paw, 108–10, *110,* 172

Monster Pit, 126, 129

Monster Pit Key, 112, 126–27, *127*

Morrissey, 146

Mothers Against Drunk Driving (MADD), 42

Motive-Quest, 87

MTV, 40, 71, 77, 147

MTV Video Music Awards, 3, 108, 145, 146, 148

Murphy amendment, 146

Music Matters Asia Conference, 31

National Alliance to End Homelessness (NAEH), 125

National Defense Authorization Act, 146

National Equality March, 146

Nelson, Eric, 75

Net Promoter Score, 174, 175

New Kids on the Block, 15

*New York,* 14

New York, N.Y., 11–12, 40–41, 71, 72, 74, 129, 169

*New York Times,* 63, 72

New York University, 12

Nike, 117–18

Oakland Raiders, 116

Obama, Barack, 46, 147

O'Brien, Tom, 87–88

Office Depot, 51

One Percenters, 18, 19, 24–27, *24,* 29–30, 32–33, 73, 126, 130, 143, 165–76

as customer evangelists, 25–26

giving a name to, 82, 93–104, 170–71

as rock stocks, 123–39, 173–74

*Oprah,* 118

Osbourne, Kelly, 151

Osbourne, Ozzy, 151

"Paparazzi," 17

Pareto principle, 25

PEMCO Insurance, 133, *134*
Perry, Katy, 27
PETA, 145
Phone a Monster, 124–25
Pinterest, 28, 130
*Pittsburgh Post-Gazette*, 115
Pittsburgh Steeler's Terrible Towel, 113, 114–16, *115*, 119
"Poker Face," 17, *95*
Polamalu, Troy, 116
Polk Automobile Loyalty Award, 88
pornography, 50
Powell, Bonnie Azab, 59–60
Powers, Stephen, 63
Presley, Elvis, 39
PriceWaterhouseCoopers, 132
Procter & Gamble, 56
PropaGaga.com, 27
*Purple Cow* (Godin), 143
Pussycat Dolls, 15

Queen, 14

Rashid, Karim, 62
reddit, 28
RedOne, 16
Reichheld, Fred, 174
Reid, Harry, 146, 147
Rihanna, 27
Robb, Walter, 59–60
Rock and Roll Hall of Fame, 148
Rodemeyer, Alyssa, 46
Rodemeyer, Jamey, 45–46
*Rolling Stone*, 17
Rutledge-Borger, Meredith, 148
Ryan, Eric, 62, 64, 65

St. Pierre, Jacques, 47–49
Samuels, Bill, Jr., 97–98, 100
Samuels family, 97, 100

Sanford C. Bernstein & Company, 63
Satmetrix 2012 Net Promoter Benchmark Study, 22
*Saturday Night Live*, 80, 116
S. C. Johnson, 63
*Seattle Weekly*, 16
Sebelius, Kathleen, 46
*Selling the Dream* (Kawasaki), 38
Semerari, Renato, 150
Servicemembers Legal Defense Network, 146
Sheeran, Corey, 39–40
Shiny New Object syndrome, 21, 22
Sim, Gary, *127*
Sinatra, Frank, 39
Sinek, Simon, 37, 52–55, *52*, 63
SiriusXM, 12
*60 Minutes*, 144
Smith, Janet, 37
social media, 5, 28–30, 49, 78, 123, 130–32, 159–60
   *see also specific social media websites*
*Social Network, The*, 28
Sony/ATV, 15
Spears, Britney, 15
spotlight gifts, 129–30
Springsteen, Bruce, 128
*Stain Removal 101*, 64
stakeholder philosophy, 59, 60
Staples Center, 153
*Start with Why: How Great Leaders Inspire Everyone to Take Action* (Sinek), 52
Stengel, Jim, 56–57, 65
Stengel 50, 56, 57
Stern, Howard, 12–13
Super Bowl, 116
SXSW, 158, 159

symbols:
   sharing of, 107–20, 172–73
   turning experience into, 111–13

TARP Worldwide, 23
tattoos, 95, 111, 112, *113*
Taylor (Method customer), 64
*Telegraph, The* (London), 12
"Telephone," 17
*Time,* 3, 46, 146
Time Warner Cable, 22–23
Tisch School of the Arts, 12, 14
Tokyo Park Hyatt, 13
*Tonight Show, The,* 152
Tour de France, 118
Tuil, Yael, 149
Tumblr, 4, 43, 80
Twitter, 4, 27, 29, 30, 51, 73, 123,
   130, 136, 144, 160

unicorns, 110–11

values, 37–38, 39, 42, 57, 58, 59,
   61–62, 168–69

VH1, 3
Virgin Mobile, 125
   Freefest campaign, 125
Vitan, Donna, 160
Viva Glam, 71
*Vogue,* 149

Wagner, Mike, 116
Walmart, 84
Warhol, Andy, 15–16, 108
Whitman, Meg, 137–38
Whole Foods Market, 58–61
Winfrey, Oprah, 3, 6, 40–41, 46,
   49
*Wired,* 28
WTAE, 114

Yahoo, 82
Yezak, Ryan James, 80
YouTube, 4, 6, 13, 32, 45, 78, 79,
   81, 84, 109, 123, 136, 138

# ABOUT THE AUTHOR

Jackie Huba is the coauthor of two books on customer loyalty: *Creating Customer Evangelists: How Loyal Customers Become a Volunteer Sales Force* explains how companies convert customers into evangelists who spread the word about products, benefits, or value propositions. *Creating Customer Evangelists* has been translated into six languages and has become a strategic focus for companies around the world. Jackie's second book, *Citizen Marketers: When People are the Message*, documents the emerging world of social media and how brands should begin to embrace a participatory culture. Besides being widely used at companies as an introduction to social media, *Citizen Marketers* has been adopted by college instructors as a tool for understanding the underlying nature of social media and what it means for marketing and public relations.

Named as one of the ten most influential online marketers, Jackie coauthors the award-winning *Church of the Customer* blog. With more than 105,000 daily readers, it's ranked as one of the most popular business blogs in the world. Her work has frequently been featured in the media, such as the *The Wall*

*Street Journal, The New York Times, BusinessWeek,* and *Advertising Age.* She was a founding Board Member of the Word of Mouth Marketing Association.

She is an eleven-year veteran of IBM, a graduate of Penn State University, a Pittsburgh Steelers fanatic, and resides in Austin, Texas.

*Find out what she's up to next at jackiehuba.com.*

*You can find her on Twitter @jackiehuba.*